Brian Kelly is an exciting new astrologer, who began his career in the world of broadcasting. He has worked full time as a BBC radio producer and presenter in local radio, and has made frequent appearances on Radio 1 FM.

He gained his qualifications from the Sheila Geddes Astrological College in 1982, becoming, at the age of twenty, the youngest professional astrologer in the country. He has been teaching astrology himself since 1985.

Brian travels extensively throughout the UK, promoting astrology as a valuable counselling and predictive tool, and set up Brian Kelly Fairs in 1986, an organization which promotes intuitive, psychic, spiritual, philosophical and ecological issues. Brian believes that we can always improve our situations and quality of life, and that all it often takes is a little more self-awareness. With his incorporation of New Age beliefs into astrology, Brian brings a very modern approach to a subject that has been around for at least 6,000 years.

SCORPIO

23 OCTOBER – 21 NOVEMBER

1995

BRIAN KELLY

PAN BOOKS
LONDON, SYDNEY AND AUCKLAND

First published 1994 by Pan Books Ltd
a division of Pan Macmillan Publishers Limited
Cavaye Place, London SW10 9PG
and Basingstoke

Associated companies throughout the world

ISBN 0 330 33219 8

1 3 5 7 9 8 6 4 2

A CIP catalogue record for this book is available from the British Library

Typeset by Parker Typesetting Service, Leicester
Printed and bound in Great Britain by
Cox & Wyman Ltd, Reading, Berkshire

Contents

Chapter One

AN INTRODUCTION TO ASTROLOGY

Hello and welcome to your astrological forecast for 1995. In this book we will be covering all of the major, and most of the important minor trends which will affect your sun sign in 1995.

I believe astrology to be an invaluable tool for understanding both personality and the paths that our lives follow. As well as guiding you through the good and not so good times in the year ahead, this book includes sections on the character and lifestyle that are typical of your sign. If you have always wondered how true to type you are, read on and find out.

I intend this book to be an astrological guide to 1990s living, and to go beyond old-fashioned fortune-telling. I hope you enjoy it.

For those who are newcomers to astrology, let me briefly explain how it works. Astrology is a science of symbolism, meaning that when a particular planet appears to be in a particular place in the sky, certain events seem to be common. The concept is similar to, say, palmistry, where the lines of the palm are supposed to indicate events in the life of the individual. The lines themselves have no power but they seem to correlate with actual events and personal characteristics.

The basis of astrology involves the apparent planetary positions as viewed from Earth. Each of the eight planets in our solar system revolve around the sun. They all move at varying speeds, from a full orbit in ten months (Mercury) to a full orbit in 250 years (Pluto). As they move around the sun they appear to pass through the star constellations (though in fact they are many light years away). Early humankind believed that the stars were lights from heaven, twinkling through holes in the blackness, and that the planets were gods and goddesses who had their places and paths in the firmament. The planets are therefore named after Greek and Roman mythological heroes.

The twelve star signs are derived from groups of stars (the constellations), each of which represents one-third of each of the four seasons. Stories and myths about the constellations grew up over the centuries, as observers on earth imagined their lives to be influenced by the stars' powers. The stars Castor and Pollux, for example, were named by the Romans after mythological twin brothers who they believed had been immortalized as stars in the sky to protect humankind in their day-to-day activities and when travelling. These stars relate to the star sign Gemini (the sign of the twins) and Gemini people are well-known for their constant movement and activity.

These days we don't, as the Romans might have done, send up prayers to Castor and Pollux to protect us when we are travelling, and we don't really believe that the planets and stars have any powers of their own. One way of looking at astrology is to regard the planetary move-ments as a mirror which reflects the mood of the moment and which can inform us as to when is a propitious time to take a certain action, such as travel for instance – advice which we can either take or leave.

Astrologers look at the planets – Mercury, Venus, Mars, Jupiter, Saturn, Uranus, Neptune and Pluto – and also observe three other bodies – the Sun, the Moon and the 'new' planet or comet Chiron.

The sun is the centre of our solar system. It is station-ary, but when we look up at the sky it seems to move. We talk about 'sunrise' and 'sunset' and the sun being 'overhead at noon'. The sun never actually moves, but in astrological (Earth-centred) terms it does (hence sunrise and sunset). When you talk about your 'star sign', you are referring to your sun sign – the sign in front of which the sun appeared to be during the month of your birth. The orbit of the Earth around the sun is so regular that the sun always appears to be in the same place on the same date each year. For example, if you were born on 1 February you would always be an Aquarian, regardless of which year it was. Each sun sign begins and ends, therefore, on more or less the same date each year, so by knowing someone's birthday alone, one can know what sun sign they belong to. All general astrological forecasts are based on what's called 'Sun-sign' Astrology, where astrologers take everyone to be a typical representative of the sign and make forecasts from the starting point.

Although your birthdate dictates your sign, there are twelve different ways of expressing the energy represented by the sign. This energy is influenced by your 'Ascendant' or 'rising' sign which depends on the time of day you were born. Throughout the twenty-four hours of the Earth's revolution, the pattern of stars visible from a set point changes as different constellations are faced at different times. All twelve signs of the zodiac 'rise' throughout the day, so depending upon your time of birth, a particular star sign (any of the twelve) will be rising. The characteristics of that sign will be evident in your personality.

You may find that many of the people closest to you belong to a star sign which is generally considered to be incompatible with your own, yet you get on well with them. They might have your ascendant sign as their sun sign. A person who is better known for her ascendant sign personality than her sun sign personality is the Duchess of York. She's a Libra sun sign – the sign of peace, harmony and co-operation – but her ascendant sign is Scorpio – the sign of passion, intensity and conviction.

There is another sign of the zodiac which can be highly influential in our lives and that is the sign in which the moon was placed when we were born. The moon orbits the Earth in twenty-eight days. During this period it spends just over two days in each star sign – taking twenty-eight days 'to complete'. When you were born the moon could have been in any of the twelve signs. Next to the sun sign, and more importantly than the ascendant sign, the moon sign is crucial when examining the personality of the individual. As an example, Michael Jackson is a sun sign Virgo, making him particular, fastidious and a perfectionist. His moon sign, indicating his emotional life, is in Pisces, the sign of sensitivity, gentleness, innocence and isolation. Can you see how it works in his life?

We will talk throughout the book about the moon, and how it affects us on a very personal level, and in Chapter 9 you will discover where the moon is every day this year and what its position might mean to you.

Chiron

In Pasadena, California, in November 1977, a new heavenly body was discovered. It has subsequently been named Chiron, after the centaur of mythology, who was a weapon maker and healer.

The discovery of a 'new' planet generates great excitement in astronomical and astrological circles. The scientists want to analyse it, dissect it, plot its orbit and speed and we intuitives say, 'What does it mean?' There seems to be some disagreement as to whether Chiron is a planet or a comet, but if it isn't a planet as we know it, it may just be the broken remnants of a planet. It has an orbit within our solar system and is nearer to us than Uranus, Neptune or Pluto.

What does the first potential planet since Pluto in 1930 mean to modern humankind? I call it the planet of health and environmentalism – both subjects which have risen to prominence in recent years. Its discovery has coincided with increased interest in vegetarianism, and awareness of the danger of food additives, global warming, and the threats to the rain forests. The discovery of a planet always ties in with a change in the thinking on Earth. Pluto's energies of mass power were symbolized through the development of atomic weapons and the increase of Communism and Fascism. Before that, the discovery of the planet of rebellion, Uranus, in the 1780s, coincided with revolutions in industry and France, to name but two.

Chiron also seems to influence the area of computers and technology. People with the planet strongly placed tend to have quite far-thinking minds, and often a special ability to invent things or understand the logical processes of the computer programme or video game.

If it is to have keyword characteristics, Chiron is to do with a search for truth, for purity, for honesty, for reality, for health, for hope, for the self and for meaning in life. Astrologers like to assign heavenly bodies to particular star signs, and I'm no exception. I like the way that Chiron seems to be similar to the sign Virgo. Look at the above characteristics and see how they relate to friends or relatives whose sun sign is Virgo!

I will talk about Chiron in this book. This is possibly the first time that Chiron has been given credit in this type of forecast book and I hope that by the end of the year you will agree with me that it is too influential to be ignored.

I hope you enjoy reading and using this book. It will be useful when it comes to making the most of any successful period, or for accepting that the time is not quite right for particular activities and for finding out a little more about who you are and where you are heading.

Chapter Two

READING
YOUR
HOROSCOPE

As you will no doubt know, astrology is based on much more than just your sun sign characteristics. Your horoscope, or birth chart, will tell an astrologer everything about you, often down to the finest details. In this section, you will find three horoscopes of well-known celebrities who share your sun sign. As we look closer at their birth charts, we will see how each is very different, and how the subtle placings of the planets 'in' particular signs and astrological houses will influence the individual personalities.

Obviously, we will not be able to look in depth at the horoscopes of each person, so what we will do is to use three factors to interpret the personality: the sun sign, the moon sign, and the ascendant sign.

How the Signs and Planets Affect Your Personality

Your sun sign, as we have seen, is the sign through which the sun appeared to be passing in the month you were born. This sign has the greatest effect on your character, but is modified by your moon sign, the sign through which the moon was passing at this time, and your ascendant sign or rising sign. This is the constellation which was rising on the eastern horizon at the time that you were born. Each of the twelve star signs 'rises' every day. Your ascendant sign will be any of the twelve and will depend upon what time of day you were born. If you do not know your birth time, you may not ever be sure of your ascendant sign. If you do know your birth time, there are astrological books available which will show you how to write it out. Your ascendant sign will describe the way in which you lead your life.

The twelve houses are sections of the sky, each one ruling a different part of everyday life. They are unequal in size, and look like segments of an orange, the sky being conceived of as a sphere. The position of the planets in the houses at the time of your birth also influences your personality.

In order to understand how your moon and ascendant signs affect your horoscope you need to know what each sign and planet stands for.

The Signs

ARIES is the sign of energy and physical actions. ♈

TAURUS is the sign of sensuality and material things. ♉

GEMINI is the sign of variety, words and information. ♊

CANCER is the sign of tenacity and emotional needs. ♋

LEO is the sign of creativity and performance. ♌

VIRGO is the sign of analysis and work. ♍

LIBRA is the sign of agreement and relationships. ♎

SCORPIO is the sign of power and passion. ♏

SAGITTARIUS is the sign of extremes and adventures. ♐

CAPRICORN is the sign of discipline and status. ♑

AQUARIUS is the sign of invention and friendliness. ♒

PISCES is the sign of sacrifices and dreams. ♓

The Planets

MERCURY = Communication and information ☿

VENUS = Love and tastes ♀

MARS = Vitality and drive ♂

JUPITER = Enjoyment and philosophy ♃

SATURN = Lessons and rules ♄

CHIRON = Awareness and effort ⚷

URANUS = Originality and independence ♅

NEPTUNE = Illusions and beliefs ♆

PLUTO = Power and undercurrents ♇

Celebrity Horoscopes

Armed with all the information of this section, let us now look at the personalities of our three celebrities.

HRH The Prince of Wales
Sun in Scorpio, Moon in Taurus, Ascendant Leo

Scorpios are all passionate and Charles's passion falls in the area of the horoscope which rules pleasure. His love life will always have been a strong driving force. The Sun's placing next to Chiron means that his passion leads to self-discovery through the development of awareness. Does this mean that he learns about himself through his love life and leisure interests?

The Moon in Taurus indicates stability and emotional consistency, and its particular placing near its north nodal point is an indication of popularity and a life in the public eye.

Kingly Leo rising is to be expected in the chart of a royal. It is also often seen in the charts of people who are assertive.

Forecast for 1995

Charles has to change and this year will see him doing so. His role in the world and in the Royal Family will undergo a transformation that he has known was coming for a long time. It will be seen as him finally asserting his personality after years of being overshadowed by protocol and tradition. There will be much negotiation as he attempts to establish his position, and he will have to fight for what he wants.

Love will rear a rather controversial head this year and, following an occasion in a foreign country, there will have to be some sort of announcement.

Roseanne Arnold
Sun in Scorpio, Moon in Gemini, Ascendant Aquarius

Passion lies wherever in the chart a Scorpio's Sun in Scorpio is to be found. Roseanne's Sun in Scorpio is in the area of the chart that governs freedom, philosophy and morals – which may explain her tendency to be a law unto herself and rather outspoken.

Gemini Moon people are always able to adapt to a changing world, and having her Moon in the domestic part of the chart means that Roseanne is able to identify very strongly with the psychological imprints that we subtly receive from our families. Perhaps her own traumatic early life has led her to portray a character in a domestic set-up – as a way of bringing humour to bear on some of the everyday problems that crop up in the life of a family.

Aquarius is often rising in the charts of those who appeal to a wide variety of people and who have a slightly controversial image.

Forecast for 1995

It looks as though the popular show *Roseanne* will come to the end of its natural life this year. As a result, she will need a time of reassessment prior to deciding where to go from here. There will be many guest appearances on other people's shows, but an international tour may be rejected in favour of spending more time at home with her family. In many ways, Roseanne will come out of the change more successfully than is expected.

Whoopi Goldberg
Sun in Scorpio, Moon in Scorpio, Ascendant Aquarius

The Sun and Moon in the same sign indicate a person who is very aware of what and who she is, and it gives Whoopi Goldberg a double dose of passion. An emphasis on the part of the chart that rules independence and morals indicates that she will have strong views, and that she will be interested in breaking down barriers. Saturn next to the Sun suggests that she has had to learn some hard lessons in life – perhaps through being exposed to prejudice.

Her Scorpio Moon is next to Mercury and this is always seen in the charts of people who can think and feel at the same time, and in the chart of an actress can lead to a true empathy with the feelings of the characters she portrays.

Aquarius rising has brought her popularity and a slightly controversial image.

Forecast for 1995

This is a big year for Ms Goldberg's career. She may become one of the highest paid Hollywood actresses for her role in a love story which crosses all sorts of boundaries. The role will have a number of psychological undercurrents as well as a strong moral message. This year may go down as one of Whoopi's finest.

Chapter Three

THE WORLD
THIS
YEAR

There will be a more 'feel good' atmosphere throughout the world in 1995 and many countries in which there has been tension in previous years will have a noticeable change of attitude. Improvements will be seen in the former Yugoslavia, for example. As always, though, the year will have its fair share of interesting political and other developments.

The Countries

The United Kingdom will have a year of great national pride. The British Royal Family will be in the news, but for all the right reasons. Expect to see a great State occasion. There could be an important wedding. The money supply will be the best it has been for years, and it will be tempting to say that 'we've never had it so good' (this decade at least). The ordinary person will feel well-off, and the Government will benefit from a wave of popularity. There will be a boom in the property market, with a lot of talk about people purchasing second homes. On the down side, a much publicized relationship, possibly a showbiz couple or perhaps royalty, will finally come to an end, and there will be some kind of tragedy involving water transport.

The United States will have a turbulent year, and the Administration will have to make some difficult decisions, especially with regard to the Third World, as well as on domestic social issues. Critical fingers will point at those in power and there will be accusations of the wealthy living a high life whilst the poor suffer. International sympathy will extend to a group of women fighting a lone cause. A dramatic solution to the employment situation will be mooted and the gamble may pay off.

There will be a change of government and leader in Cuba in 1995. It may not be unexpected but the level of upheaval will catch many by surprise.

Australia will have a turning-point year. There may be changes to the constitution, which will give the nation a new identity and on many occasions this year the eyes of the world will be focused on this country. In sport or adventure, someone from Australia will win a special award and will talk about the antipodean spirit. On the less pleasant side there will be increasing talk about skin cancer, caused by harmful sun's rays, and health as an issue will be much discussed following the death of a celebrity figure as a result of the AIDS virus.

New Zealand will have a change of government in 1995, and the way that it comes about will be sudden and controversial. There could be allegations of greed and corruption. This is a year of great self-analysis for this country, and it may choose a change of image.

Canada will lose something or someone important in 1995, and events may move swiftly at the end of the year as the change takes place. There may be unrest; rioting in the streets is not an impossibility. Unemployment may be of increasing concern in this country and this is likely to lead to reforms which will not be popular in right-wing circles.

South Africa is in for a tough year. There is every possibility that the government will fall or resign and there will be waves of unrest throughout the year. Many people may feel powerless to act as those who feel themselves to have been oppressed will make some tough demands. Out of the turmoil a new government should rise, but it will be something very unlike that which the world has been used to there, to date.

In Africa, there will be good news for Zimbabwe – in contrast to that of its neighbour South Africa. The end of the year will bring a freer and much more positive outlook for all groups within.

Difficulties will affect a usually quiet West African country when a disaster has a high human cost.

The United Nations will have a struggle on more than one occasion in 1995. Third World countries will have much to say about a so-called narrow outlook within the organization, and it may come to a particular woman to make the right comments to defuse the situation. A very old country, possibly with a royal family, will have to be brought into line when it asks for special treatment unacceptable to most members. The signing of a new agreement in the autumn will finally sort out problems which have been troublesome in one part of the world for some time.

The EC will be in a strong position in 1995 and new member states may take steps to join. As usual, the UK will be seen to be dragging its heels when new financial plans are put forward but the plans may receive a tricky reception in more than one quarter. New agreements will be signed and a document will prove to be historic. A farming country will become a headache for those wishing to see progress, but by the autumn it will have been possible to persuade them to accept reform.

Former Communist countries will be in the news in 1995. Albania will be going through financial and territorial problems which may result in a part of the population feeling ignored. The Baltic States will have one of the success stories of the year when a person in the Arts world receives international acclaim. Hungary is in for a tricky year. It may be that the peaceful revolution of recent years will prove not to have been enough for some people and there will be political changes in this country, some of which will be said to have been much too late.

Western Europe will see a few changes. Little Belgium causes a stir when it dares to question an unquestionable subject and it makes its point quite clear. The history books may need to be researched to find out just what this unusual outburst relates to. In Greece, a domestic issue becomes the focus of a world debate and a problem in the holiday islands will concern many. There could be a change of government when some kind of administrative problem gets right out of hand. Turkey will also see big changes in 1995. There may also be a change of government here, and the whole country enters into a new period of history – starting in the spring. Turkish-occupied Northern Cyprus is likely to see international recognition this year following years of stalemate between past Greek and Turkish governments.

Arab countries will be in the news – Egypt, because it takes a much more Western approach in many of its dealings, especially those involving Israel, and also when a compromise is actively sought regarding an important domestic question. A territorial question arises in Saudi Arabia and there may be tension in certain religious quarters. Oil prices may rise as a result.

Arts and Sports in 1995

The Arts world will be dominated by a revival of horror and macabre themes. Expect to see plenty of films which make your flesh creep. Mummies will make a comeback, and people will be talking about ancient Egyptian curses. There will be romance and sentimentality as well, but it may be tinged with cynicism. The religious epic as a work of art will return in the shape of a remake of a classic movie – except this time, the story will be told as realistically as possible. Travel films will also be big and there will be an increasing wanderlust as people see their favourite stars in exotic locations and wish that they, too, were there.

The world of dance will be highlighted early in the year as will the world of opera. An Italian opera singer makes a great impact, and the dance influences come from a country of natural charm but little sophistication.

On the sporting front, team events will be suffering from behind-the-scenes reorganization. Few major sports will escape. Expect to see fundamental changes discussed in soccer, cricket and American football. Winter sports will be increasingly popular, especially skiing and ice-skating. Being fit will become a national sport in many countries and there will be a number of reports about why we should keep active. New health scares about heart disease may frighten people into taking up exercise. Records will be broken this year – especially regarding anything to do with jumping or climbing or sailing long distances, and one particular pairing or partnership will capture the imagination of the world.

In the Headlines

January will see a special achievement, possibly in the sporting field.
An old dictator will make something of a comeback.

17

An important legal/contractual matter will be discussed between two governments as the question of old territorial rights comes up again.

A fire will devastate a place of work somewhere in the former Eastern Bloc.

February will be full of delays and cancellations and a large event will have to be postponed, affecting many people.

Social deprivation will be a talking point.

Someone famous, possibly a previously well-respected politician, will be shown up in their true colours as someone who puts money before love.

March will see the Church making a moral point. There will be much in the way of discussion about 'proper' behaviour, and people will talk of hypocrisy.

A powerful figure will exercise some kind of cruelty but little can be done about it.

There may be a climbing or mountain accident.

A charity may be in trouble with money.

April will see a complicated legal case, and the possible imprisonment of a public figure.

A high-profile person with a glamorous image may stand accused of a misdemeanour.

There may be a disaster connected to fire and the sea.

May will be quite a violent month, with fighting erupting in a volatile part of the world.

An adventurer, or daredevil, will embark upon an exercise that many feel is ill-advised.

An Asian army will be in the news, with some kind of celebration or public show of strength.

A drowning accident will shock many.

June will see a batch of forest fires.

An industrial dispute or political drama will break out

when an engineering group tries to repair damage caused by war or neglect.

A new law to prevent exploitation at work will come into force in the Far East.

July will see a spectacular entertainment failure in public.

A disaster which affects an entire town will rouse the world.

The Arts will be in the news when someone with a specific literary skill makes everyone take notice.

The calendar will contain a major social event that many will say is a waste of time and money.

August will see extremes of weather. It will be particularly hot in many places, but there may be a hurricane or strong wind which causes damage.

Buildings will collapse, possibly as a result of the strong climatic conditions.

There will be more than one international celebrity death – probably a female film star and someone of religious significance.

September will contain an intrigue which becomes a much bigger scandal as time goes by. It is likely to involve large-scale crime.

There will be some kind of drama underground.

A legal case will eventually grind to a stalemate and a government department will be able to claim only a hollow victory.

October will see the signing of significant contracts which will unite old enemies.

An old government in a beautiful country, known for its relaxed laws, will fall, making way for a new broom to sweep clean.

Religious fervour will hit a new high.

November will see a rags-to-riches story when a self-made artist and socialite tells their story to the world.

A legal case or diplomatic incident will end in enormous costs for a Caribbean country.

More than one celebrity will be honoured for their achievements – one in the Arts, possibly design or video, and one a pioneer in Third World aid.

An aggressive woman will take the world by storm.

Race-car driving will be in the news, either with the staging of a spectacular event or some kind of new machine hitting the track.

December will bring a question about a famous building.

A food scandal will erupt following some kind of poisoning.

Disease and famine will be in the news, there will be talk of some sort of plague.

A famous person will have an accident while travelling.

A Middle-Eastern government will fall just before Christmas.

Chapter Four

FASHION
AND
THE STARS

The world of fashion relies on constant change. It is said that what we wear in the street is decided on the catwalks of Paris and Milan two years before. Astrology looks at this differently.

There are certain planetary influences which seem to have a strong bearing on long-term fashion trends. The movements of the planet Neptune, for example, seem to coincide with changes in the mood of the country, and consequently the type of clothes we like to be seen in. Neptune changes signs every fourteen to fifteen years, and when it does, our styles of dress seem to move on.

In 1984 Neptune entered Capricorn, and since then, it has been considered to be the epitome of style to be seen in the Capricorn mode of dressing – smart suits, tailoring, plain, dark colours, and the minimum of ostentation.

Previously, when Neptune was in Sagittarius, from 1971 to 1984, exaggeration was the name of the game, with platforms, wide collars, baggy trousers and long hemlines. If a Sagittarian can go too far, they will.

If you enjoyed the 1960s fashions at the time, you were appreciating Neptune in Scorpio (1957–71), which meant that we could expose ourselves in short skirts, tight trousers, see-through outfits, and striking make-up. Scorpio rules sex and impact.

After World War II, there was a craving for romance, which was reflected in the Neptune in Libra fashions of

1943–57. Shapes were full, colours were prominent, and party clothes were the thing of the moment. Libra is the sign of romance and party-time.

It is sometimes difficult to separate one year from the others as being significant, but there are always subtle changes, which indicate a constant development in the style of dressing. This chapter looks at the fashions we can expect to wear in 1995, and we will also talk about the shape and style which suits your star sign, and those of your friends and family.

Overall Style for the Year

As previously mentioned, Capricorn continues to be the background in fashion at the moment, so you are still wise to purchase a sensible 'interview' suit, in navy or grey, and to make sure that the tailoring is fairly severe, so that you look well turned-out when shopping in the fashionable high street. The suit is the language of respectability in 1995 as in most of the past ten years.

Your underwear will need to be a little more upmarket this year. Try going for silk and *broderie anglaise*.

Make-up will be more pronounced this year, and you'll find that you can be more adventurous with your lipstick. Your earrings may need to be more delicate.

Colours to wear in 1995 are black, grey, navy, purples, gold, blue and green. Avoid reds, pinks and pastels.

Much less change is apparent in the men's styles of any one year and the smart clothes which we have all been wearing for ten years are still the main theme. If, however, you are investing in a suit that you wish to last a while, don't choose anything with narrow legs, narrow revers and a snug fit – go for baggier and wider.

If you wish to be a streetwise cool dude in 1995, you'll have to invest in baggier jeans, huge tops and some kind of hat – possibly of ethnic origin.

Pockets will be fashionable in 1995, and may move around. There may be a return to the hipster pockets of the 1970s.

Shoes will be big, with possibly a slight platform, and you may also be able to dig out your old Jesus sandals.

What has been noticeable over the past two or three years is that the narrowness of lapel, tie and trouser has given way to a wider and softer looking shape. We will not see a return to the 1970s 'baggies', but trousers and skirts need not now be as leg-hugging as before.

Cocktail and party wear for women has not changed much in recent years. To be totally 'with it' in 1995 you need to bring in flowers and flowery patterns. Hemlines continue to be long, it will not be considered stylish to show your knees.

Jackets, this year, will be hip length. The waist has almost totally disappeared in the last couple of years. Blouses will be in soft colours, more feminine, and in silky fabrics.

If your waist disappears, your cleavage may become more apparent and necklines are plunging this year. The fuller figure is also back – no straight-up-and-down types on the catwalk this year. However, you will need to keep up the exercising in 1995, as many of the styles, though full, will drape across you, showing what's underneath.

Another tip for 1995, especially in the colder weather, involves an accessory – the snood or shawl. Both, if worn over a business suit, will create a shape for the year.

Hair will be longer this year, and more feminine. You may see more people letting it hang loosely.

Street fashion will continue to show a mystical influence but with more African and Indian-style motifs. There may also be a return to the overalls-influenced styles of the late 1970s and uniforms may make a comeback.

You and Your Clothes

If you're true to the characteristics of your sign, what will your style be? The following is a guide to dressing for your sign, including what NOT to do.

ARIES – Looks good in styles which allow fast movement. You will thoroughly enjoy the all-in-one sporty suits of 1995. You are at home in jeans, but you can create an impact when dressing in tailoring so sharp you'd cut yourself on it.
Colours – Reds, but in 1995, try wearing more black and gold.
NEVER NEVER wear anything too tight, or a wall of one colour that could stun an ox at a hundred paces.

TAURUS – Looks for the fabric first, style second. It's so important to feel comfortable in your clothes, so you make sure you feel the quality first. You may not have thousands of outfits, but what you do have is good taste. You like the lower necklines this year, and will enjoy experimenting with necklaces and scarves.
Colours – Browns and greens, both acceptable in 1995. Use more gold this year.
NEVER NEVER go out in something as old as Methuselah just because 'it's comfortable'.

GEMINI – Looks so young for so long, it's almost sinful. You can get away with street fashion well into your forties. If you have the legs, go for the 'twiggy' look. Men can dress as boys with great success.
Colours – Yellows, but not this year. Try going for gold, a little purple, and lots more blue.
NEVER NEVER wear 'cheap and cheerful' if you don't want to end up looking 'past it and poor'.

CANCER – Looks like one of your parents, and suits their

sort of outfit. You like tradition, so why should you give up wearing your baggy pullies and voluminous frocks? In fact, your natural style is quite acceptable this year. Buy classic and you can't go wrong.

Colours – Pinks, lemons and most pastels. You too need more gold and black to look with it.

NEVER NEVER wear what you'd wear at home in the street – it'd frighten the horses.

LEO – Looks are so important to the glamour queen/king of the zodiac. You really can't miss out on all the tailoring this year. Treat every day as though you are about to be selected as the managing director.

Colours – Gold and sunny colours. You could venture into purple if you were daring, as you usually are!

NEVER NEVER wear so much jewellery that magpies swoop on you and drivers are dazzled by the glow.

VIRGO – Looks at their reflection in every shop window. You are obsessed about every dangling thread and unnecessary crease, so go for severe tailoring in colours that won't show the dirt. Avoid anything too trendy – you'd feel odd and would keep pulling at it.

Colours – White and creams. OK in 1995, but you could try to introduce green.

NEVER NEVER wear non-crease man-made fabrics. Sloppiness doesn't become you.

LIBRA – Looks the prettiest of all the signs. Most things look good on you, and you'll have an especially attractive year, dressed in flowers, bright colours and flowing styles. Romance is back – you smell and taste gorgeous.

Colours – Blues, greens and pinks. The first two will look even more stunning if mixed with greys.

NEVER NEVER wear everything to match – frock, handbag, hat, shoes . . . you could be mistaken for wallpaper.

SCORPIO – Looks like something from a vampire or steamy movie. You like to make an impact, which is why your outfits are always so dramatic. You could experiment with the ethnic styles this year to create a new interesting image. Colours – Black and red. Try black and purple this year for even more mystery.
NEVER NEVER try to jolly up your appearance. You'll end up looking like Cruella de Ville dressed as Pinocchio.

SAGITTARIUS – Looks are never that important to the adventurer of the zodiac. This year, however, you seem to have stumbled across all your favourite styles. Lots of sporty clothes and you love the baggy shapes. You'll buy big, clumping shoes.
Colours – Purples and golds – both the height of fashion in 1995. You will be the belle/beau of the ball.
NEVER NEVER wear the same crumpled outfit day after day. You may not mind, but others will think you're a mess.

CAPRICORN – Looks for just the 'right' thing to wear, and it could take months. The Capricorn appearance is always immaculate – not a hair out of place. You hate the street fashions at the moment, and would rather die than be seen without a suit and full make-up.
Colours – Blacks, greys, navy – all definitely 'in' in 1995. You could venture into green if you were daring (which mostly you aren't!).
NEVER NEVER wear a conventional suit which was conventional in 1970 and now makes you look like something from a museum.

AQUARIUS – Looks like something from another planet most of the time. You like to be different, so you'll enjoy experimenting with the fuller shapes of 1995 making up your own version of the 1990s hippy. Go for the beads and sandals in a big way.

Colours – Blues, silver and grey. Your colours do well in 1995. Try green as well if you want a contrast.

NEVER NEVER insist on wearing something from Oxfam at a society wedding. They may call the police.

PISCES – Looks like a lost soul and dresses to prove it. You love to wear up-to-the-minute fashion combined with clothes from the past, and you'll have many more hats and shoes by the end of this year. You could end up looking like a character from a Dickens novel, but so sweet with it.

Colours – Greens and blues and silver. You'll be much admired in 1995.

NEVER NEVER buy something because it looks good on your friend. At best you'll look like a clone, and at worst a sausage in the wrong skin.

Finally, a tip for 1996. Much more ethnic influence coming in – possibly from Eastern Europe.

Chapter Five

THE POSITIVE POWER OF ASTROLOGY

As we have seen, astrology can be used to learn more about ourselves – our strengths and our weaknesses. Now, for the first time in a forecast book, we are going to utilize this self-knowledge and, together with the New Age techniques of Visualization and Affirmation, learn how to arrive at a clear idea of our true needs. We often struggle to live up to the expectations of family and friends, even of society in general, and fail to realize that in acting against our nature we are placing great stress on our shoulders. In order to release this burden we need to understand what we really want out of life.

What is Visualization?

Your mind thinks in pictures. If you believe that you are a failure, you tend to apply that belief to everything you do. Each time you find yourself in a situation where that belief becomes activated, you see a mental picture of an occasion when you feel you failed in the past, and you apply it to the event in hand. If you can concentrate on that 'failure' picture and turn it into something which is pleasant and encouraging, you have successfully Creatively Visualized. This technique is also sometimes called Creative Imagery.

What is Affirmation?

We affirm when we say to ourselves something which bolsters our confidence. You are about to make a speech at a crowded meeting, for example. You affirm when you say to yourself, 'Go on, you can do it – be dynamic, knock 'em dead.'

You may have been programmed by other people into believing certain negative things about yourself. Suppose that throughout your growing years a parent or relative had constantly told you that you were fat/ugly/stupid. It would be very difficult not to believe that they were right. If we want to regain a positive self-image, we can use the technique of affirmation – saying something to ourselves over and over again, as a way of bombarding our brain with some positive information, which, if done often enough, we eventually come to believe.

The Problem Signs

Let's start by looking at the astrological element to which your sun sign belongs. It may be that one of the other elements is not well represented in your natal horoscope, and that you have problems relating to its energy.

The Fire signs are Aries, Leo, Sagittarius. Vitality is not usually a problem to Fire, but you may find yourself lacking in practical ability and realism (Earth), ideas and logic (Air), or sensitivity and caring (Water). Too much Fire, however, could make you over-excitable and demanding.

The Earth signs are Taurus, Virgo, Capricorn. Being grounded is not usually a problem to Earth, but you may find yourself lacking in enthusiasm and spirit (Fire), ideas and logic (Air), or sensitivity and caring (Water). Too much Earth, however, could make you over-materialistic and sceptical.

The Air signs are Gemini. Libra, Aquarius. Communication is not usually a problem to Air, but you may find yourself lacking in enthusiasm and spirit (Fire), practical ability and realism (Earth), or sensitivity and caring (Water). Too much Air, however, could make you over-cerebral and gossipy.

The Water signs are Cancer, Scorpio, Pisces. Feeling is not usually a problem to Water, but you may find yourself lacking in enthusiasm and spirit (Fire), practical ability and realism (Earth), or ideas and logic (Air). Too much water, however, could make you over-emotional and erratic.

You see how you may be experiencing a difficulty with the energy of a particular element? Let us now create a visualization for changing the way the elements work within you. Do you have too much of an element, or not enough?

Fire

Not enough – Visualize striking a match and watch how the fire – your personal fire – takes hold. Imagine that the fire is the ignition of a particular project you wish to get going.
Too much – Visualize how a fire needs to be contained. Contrast a raging forest fire with a contained furnace. See how much good can be done by containing the fire.

Earth

Not enough – Visualize building a house. With each brick you lay you have helped to ground yourself a little more.
Too much – Visualize trying to run, swim or fly, carrying everything you own. You will move faster as you let go of things.

Air

Not enough – Visualize the wind. Feel how invigorating fresh air really is. It clears away all the cobwebs of the past.
Too much – Visualize an electric fan. Moving air is

refreshing but a fan with multi-speeds can be slowed down. Feel your brain slowing down in the same way.

Water

Not enough – Visualize rain falling after a drought. It is the beginning of hope and of new life.

Too much – Visualize torrential rain and floods. See the sun coming out and a rainbow forming as the clouds disappear and the water recedes.

How Can I Tell if There's Something Wrong?

It so often happens that we find ourselves in situations we feel we've been through before that we are forced to ask whether this is more than a coincidence. Could it be that it is our own behaviour which causes us to get into the same difficulties again and again? Ask yourself if the complaints listed below remind you of yourself or people you know.

ARIES
No one agrees with me.
Someone just hit me for no reason.
Why are people frightened of me?

TAURUS
Why should I change?
People always hassle me to hurry up.
How can doing something the way it's always been done be wrong?

GEMINI
I did not say what you said I said.
How dare you question my fidelity!
Can't anyone else see that black is white?

CANCER
I can't do that.

You're just using me.
No one sees my point of view.

LEO
If someone doesn't get me what I've asked for I'll scream.
Everyone must hate me.
Are you disobeying my orders?

VIRGO
I feel sick.
I can't carry on in this situation – it's intolerable.
Everyone's inadequate.

LIBRA
I have nothing to wear.
My best friend has betrayed me.
I'm trying to please everyone at once.

SCORPIO
Can't anyone see what's really the matter?
After all I've done for . . .
I can't forgive them for what they did.

SAGITTARIUS
What do you mean 'I don't listen'?
So, I wasn't there when it happened, what's the problem?
You always want me to stay at home.

CAPRICORN
You've got no class.
I won't do what's not in my job description.
This isn't in the rules.

AQUARIUS
Why are you forcing me?
This is a prison.
What a lot of boring people.

PISCES
I don't care what you do.
I'm so scared.
Why won't anyone else have another drink?

Mind and Body

There is a growing school of thought which equates physical problems to our mental state. People develop arthritis after years of feeling frustrated, cancer is thought to be caused by resentment eating away at us, heart attacks often affect people who cannot express love . . . etc. It's a controversial point of view because in our society we like to believe that we are 'victims' of illness, which just strikes us as fate decrees. The evidence grows, however, to show that happy people live longer, those with interests are more healthy, and that people who talk about their problems feel better.

We have known for a while that exercise and healthy food will keep us well, but do we follow that philosophy? Do we look after our bodies in the way that we should, or do we fill ourselves full of sweets, chocolate, cakes, biscuits, red meat, fried food, fast food . . .? There are even some cases when we deliberately do not eat enough food – as if we're saying, 'If I starve myself, someone will *have* to look after me.' Why, also, do we drink tea, coffee, cola (all full of stimulants and acid) on top of alcohol and cigarette smoking?

In many cases, our health problems are caused by the way that we neglect our emotional, physical or mental needs. Let's look at why certain parts of us might be more delicate by predisposition.

ARIES has problems with the head and general vitality. Could this be the result of plunging head first into the action and wearing themselves out?

34

TAURUS has problems in the throat and neck areas. Could this be the result of swallowing too much anger, and being afraid to turn to look in a different direction?

GEMINI could develop problems in the shoulders or the nerves. Could this be the result of feeling constantly tense and on edge?

CANCER has a sensitive chest and liver area. Could this be the result of often hunching over, or having a metaphorical, and possibly real, 'soft underbelly'?

LEO often has back problems or heart trouble. Could this be the result of feeling unsupported or insignificant?

VIRGO will have digestive disorders or eye problems. Could this be the result of having a dislike of bodily functions, and of seeing 'the truth'?

LIBRA will have teeth problems and also problems in the lower back area. Could this be the result of not wanting to cut where necessary and needing to have 'something to fall back on'?

SCORPIO will have problems with their sexual parts and sexual behaviour. Could this be because sex takes up too much of their thoughts and time?

SAGITTARIUS will have vulnerability in the joints, especially the hips. Could this be the result of living too fast and too hard?

CAPRICORN has problems with bones and skin. Could this be due to their need to maintain a veneer of calm to cover their inner turbulence?

AQUARIUS will have problems with circulation and their legs. Could this be due to their need to mix freely with all people while feeling unsupported in their aims or blocked by social pressures?

PISCES people are often allergic and they have delicate feet. Could this be because they feel too sensitive for this world and do not want to touch reality?

Now Let's Change . . .

Below I will suggest an appropriate scene for each sign. You may choose to visit an actual place which resembles the scene, or you could form a picture of that scene in your mind. Once at that point where your sun sign energy is at one with your mental picture, you can close your eyes, breathe in the atmosphere, and visualize . . .

As well as visualizations, I will include some affirmations to help change the way you think. Say your affirmations over and over to yourself, whenever you have a spare moment, until your psyche has received the message.

ARIES
Scene – An empty race-track or sports stadium.
For hyperactivity – Imagine the cars driving along the track but going slower and slower. There's no need to rush. See yourself in the winning car.
For arguments – Imagine all the cars having cushions around them. See the person you argued with and yourself just having scraped bumpers – no harm done.
For aggression – Imagine yourself after a run around the race-track. You are too tired. Being sparky doesn't matter any more.
For your head – Imagine your brain – see how delicate your head is. It is precious – surround it with blue healing light.

Affirmations:
I am no longer angry
I can achieve more if I don't rush
Every point of view is valid
My head is precious

TAURUS
Scene – A rural farm.
For greed – Each of the animals are fed in turn. The cows,

being bigger than the sheep, eat more, but no animal takes any more than they need.

For rigidity – Imagine the progress of the seasons. Each has its time and each gives way to the next when its time is up.

For the throat – Imagine each animal calling in turn. Each voice is different but they all communicate what they feel.

For the neck – Imagine that your neck could turn 360 degrees. What would you see behind you?

Affirmations:
I have everything I need at this time
Change is a natural development
I can say what I like. I speak the truth
My path is only one path
I enjoy giving

GEMINI
Scene – Your neighbourhood at 3 a.m.

For opposing views – Imagine how the night makes everything look very different to its appearance in daylight. Both pictures are true.

For trust – Imagine someone coming towards you in the dark. You know that they won't hurt you. Exchange a smile with them as they pass by – feel what it is to trust.

For the shoulders and nerves – Imagine lying on your bed in total darkness, feeling very sleepy. Feel the relaxation spreading through your body.

For boredom – Imagine how interesting it is not being able to see anything in the dark. You have to use your imagination . . .

Affirmations:
I accept responsibility for everything I say
People need me to be trustworthy, just as I need them to be so
I know the truth and speak it
I am relaxed
I use my spare time to create

CANCER

Scene – A busy children's playground.

For negativity – Imagine the hurt face of a child when you say you won't play with them. How can you turn them down?

For feeling used – Imagine what it must be like not to be needed. The child needs its mother and, in giving, she is never being used.

For feeling misunderstood – Imagine how difficult it is for one child to be heard above the others. If the child's opinions are never heard, of course they will feel misunderstood. It is up to you to get your message across.

For your chest and liver – Imagine a large pink heart being placed over your chest area. It covers you. It is love and it is strong.

For worry – As you watch the children playing on the swings, the slide, the climbing frame, you know you have to leave them be. You can't protect them for the rest of their lives, just as you can't prevent a lot of what life throws at you.

Affirmations:
I often say yes
I only do what I do with love
People know me and love me
I help each to follow their own path

LEO

Scene – The stage of an empty theatre.

For self-centredness – Imagine you are a prima donna. People may fall at your feet but until you learn to really care about others, they will not truly care for you.

For confidence – Life is a stage and you have the leading role. You won't mess it up – you're the star.

For management – Imagine being the director of the play, getting the actors to do your bidding by earning their loyalty.

For your back – Imagine you are taking acting classes. The teacher tells you how to walk: chin up, shoulders back, chest out – be proud.
For impact – Imagine the first night of a play. What sort of posters and publicity need to be on the front of the theatre?

Affirmations:
I understand the needs of others
The people who I need to love me do
I am a friend to my employees
My back is my main support

VIRGO
Scene – An immaculate town park.
For health – Imagine walking in beautifully ordered gardens. You are just one of the healthy and natural creatures there.
For panic – Imagine everything is in the place in which it is meant to be. And so are you.
For criticism – Not every flower is perfect but everything is beautiful in its own way. Who is to say what is right?
For the digestion – The processes of nature cannot be rushed. Imagine a lazy afternoon picnic on a freshly cut lawn.

Affirmations:
I enjoy being well
I only do what feels comfortable
Imperfection is natural
I digest my food with ease

LIBRA
Scene – A courtroom.
For indecision – Imagine being a judge. The public rely upon you to be able to pass judgement on a difficult case.
For being fair – Imagine how a majority verdict carries as much weight as a unanimous one. Not everyone can agree all the time.
For pleasing people – Imagine why a law is formulated. It is

for the good of the majority. How could any law be passed if the government had to please every single citizen?

For motivation – Imagine being able to put across a good case for the defence. If you sit back, you'll lose.

Affirmations:
I always come to a decision
People who love each other don't always agree
I can only be really true to my own conscience
It is good to think carefully
I know what I want to do

SCORPIO
Scene – A tunnel.

For perception – Imagine exploring the darkness. You may feel comfortable but you can understand how another person would be frightened. Accept that not everyone feels the same, and allow others to be the way they are.

For bitterness – Imagine the mountain through which the tunnel passes. Does it matter to the mountain how many trains pass through the tunnel without a word?

For forgiveness – In the dark of a tunnel many things occur which would not happen in the daylight – the rules are different. Imagine moving into the light and see if you feel the same.

For sexual problems – It is society that places such an emphasis on sex and sexual organs. Imagine that everyone is naked and see how no one part of the body is more powerful than the other.

For change – There may be darkness as we enter the tunnel but there is joy in reaching the light at the other end.

Affirmations:
My understanding is not forced on others
I do not keep scores
We all make mistakes
I am happy being sexual
Change is progress

SAGITTARIUS

Scene – An open plain.

For listening – Imagine how every sound carries in an open place and how each should be listened to carefully.

For reliability – Imagine a herd of animals. They may live on an open plain but they stay together. United they stand but divided they may fall. Feel how good it is to be needed.

For your home life – Imagine a camp fire and a barbecue. Feel the warmth of sharing with people you love.

For the joints – Imagine how each joint is lubricated and has its own strength – rather like a tree growing on the plains which can withstand wind, drought and flood.

For saying 'stop' – Imagine how even a vast plain has its limits. It can only take so much water, so many animals, so much development. There has to be a time to say 'no more'.

Affirmations:

I listen more than I talk

I am needed

I love my home

I am strong enough to know my weaknesses

I only go so far – I can stop

CAPRICORN

Scene – High above a town, on a hill.

For status – Imagine that your achievements are like a hill above a town below. Does this make you any better than the town or just different?

For pettiness – Imagine Jack and Jill climbing the hill to fetch a pail of water. Once they had fallen down, did it matter that no one had fetched any water?

For rigidity – In your town you make the rules and laws. The sheep on the hillside have not heard your rules and live in their own way. Why should they abide by rules made by people in a town?

For your body – The bones of a town are its buildings, their

41

furnishings its skin. Appreciate how both complement each other and are mutually dependent.

For achievement – Imagine the town wanting to be noticed more. If very tall buildings are erected, will the town be any better? Size is not what counts.

Affirmations:
My class is right for me, yours is for you
I adapt to the situation
Rules can be broken
I show on the outside what I am on the inside
Judge me by my actions

AQUARIUS

Scene – In a hot-air balloon, way up high.

For popularity – Imagine being a beautiful balloon sailing across the sky. People look, point, wish they were you.

For stubbornness – Imagine how a balloon has to manoeuvre itself to avoid collisions. It is not always free to stay on one course.

For feeling trapped – A balloon, when deflated, needs to be examined and repaired. It is sometimes necessary to be in touch with the ground.

For your circulation and legs – The only constant thing is progress. No balloon stays still – it must be free to move through the sky. Feel yourself being free to move.

For a more 'normal' life – Most people are in awe of a balloon, but if it was not for ordinary people, it would never have got off the ground.

Affirmations:
I am original – that's why I am so popular
Some rules must be obeyed
Reality feels good
I thrive on change
My being 'different' depends on others being the same

PISCES

Scene – A gently running stream.

For abandonment – Imagine a home-made paper yacht on the stream. If you leave it alone it will eventually sink. It needs you, don't go.

For fear – Imagine a salmon swimming against the current in order to reach its spawning ground. If something's worth doing, you can swim against the flow.

For stimulants – Imagine how ugly it is to see polluting chemicals being poured into fresh water. Will you pollute your body?

For allergies – Imagine the gentle pure water washing you clean.

For feeling unloved – Imagine Narcissus who was loved by Echo but did not know it, preferring to gaze at his own reflection in the stream. In the end Echo pined away and became just a voice. You are loved – take notice. Don't look inward, look around.

Affirmations:

Love is stronger than fear

I am capable

I do not poison my beautiful body

Allergy is fear – I am not afraid

I am loved

Chapter Six

THE
SCORPIO
PERSONALITY

General Characteristics

You are of a fluid nature, ruled by the planet of transformation, Pluto. Water signs are sensitive, sympathetic, caring and charitable. They tend to be deep, often unfathomable, and are considered to be the kindest people in the zodiac.

The planet Pluto is named after the Roman God of the Underworld (Hades in the Greek), who was the guardian of the dead – the person who had the say-so as to when people were going to join him, and who looked after them once they did. In your life you may be the kind of person others trust with really intimate and private details about themselves. You could be something of a confidant and crisis-counsellor. Your position as the eighth sign of the zodiac, double a number four – the number of security – could mean that you are able to feel secure in more than just the obvious material ways. You have the seemingly uncanny understanding of the realms of the subconscious and the spiritual world, and this gives you some kind of power, not apparent in others.

You are the only one in the zodiac who is able to see when a situation has outlived its usefulness, and when a clean break is necessary in order for progress to continue.

Appearance

If typical of your sign, you will be compact and wiry in build. Many Scorpios are very slim. If you put on weight, you'll go the whole hog and become enormous. Your colouring is either very dark, or reddish and freckly, and your eyes will be either so pale as to be nearly translucent, or nearly black. Scorpio is considered to be the sex symbol of the zodiac, so you'll know how to emphasize your assets.

Like so many other things in your life, you'll dress for effect, and that will show in contrasting colours and slightly shocking styles.

Emotionally

You are deep and intense, and so will feel things very strongly. You gain your security through being in control at all times; when you lose control, it's time for the shutters to come down all over town. Your greatest weapon is words, and you're good at putting others on the spot if you need to. Sullen phases and moodiness are characteristic, but you can't keep it up for long as you hate to be unpopular. You do know how to win friends and influence people.

Learning/Education

Scorpios are highly intuitive, often seeming to have an understanding way beyond their years. You like a structured learning situation, and your teachers will need to know a great deal about their subjects if you are to respect them. At school you were considered to be naturally talented, and you worked hard as well. Since those days you perhaps haven't used all you learned as much as you could have, but you do believe in passing on your knowledge in detail to the younger generation.

As a Child

You came into the world under unusual circumstances, and an astrological folk-tale says that a Scorpio baby is always born following a death in the family. It probably isn't true, but what is true is that your first few years definitely were out of the ordinary, and your early needs were strange. Early childhood was one of discipline and some limitation, and later on, you were made to learn the importance of putting others first, for a particular reason. Scorpio boys are gentle and deep, and the girls are often precocious.

Special Abilities

You have a special affinity for the deeper side of life – particularly religious and spiritual matters, with strong views on God. Scorpios are known for psychic and intuitive abilities, and for their excellent capabilities in a crisis.

In a Crisis

You are *the* sign for crisis management. It could be something to do with the fact that many Scorpios are made to face drama from a young age, or it could be because you understand, more than anyone, how precious and fragile security really can be. You react fast, you're not afraid of danger, and you know exactly what to say and do to minimize any damage. In some circumstances you're like a guardian angel appearing in the nick of time.

Health Matters

Your health is totally within your control. It may sound bold to say, but yours is the sign, above all others, which can wish itself better from even the most serious illness. Conversely, you're also good at wishing yourself ill, as a way of expressing strong emotional feelings. Vulnerable areas are your sexual parts, the colon and the head. You may also have some peculiar moles, or marks on your skin. As a patient you are very patient.

The Mature Years

Once you retire, you usually choose to take up some kind of social cause, and many Scorpios go into counselling at a later stage in their lives. You feel more and more political as you mature, and may wish to further ambitions in this area when you no longer need to work. Elderly Scorpios are tranquil souls, who enjoy a bottle of the hard stuff and a good book.

Family Life

Your parents possibly didn't understand you, as you were rather stubborn in pursuit of your own aims. You may have had to face adulthood at a young age for some reason. Your relationship with any brothers or sisters may have been strained, and there could have been some kind of separation. As a result, in your own family you have tried to replace the love that you felt you lost. You will give anything to your children.

Money Matters

You are the biggest business brain of the zodiac, yet you sometimes mismanage your own money. It may be because you always have your eye to the future, and sometimes forget the present. You're not above doing a shifty deal, if it will get you where you need to be, and many Scorpios keep the black economy floating. You play games with your bank, and it keeps both of you amused.

Tastes and Possessions

You can be quite possessive, and if you see something you want, you can become obsessive about it until you get it. You like big, bold items, which perhaps add something to your image. You do count the cost of what you buy, and you place a great importance on its symbolism of status. To appeal to a Scorpio an item must be dramatic and flamboyant. Your home will be one of extremes of taste.

Work and Career

You are best suited to a job which allows you scope to dig down and work out complicated matters – sometimes hidden or intimate. You enjoy being able to troubleshoot, and will find that you are often asked to fight battles for oppressed people. You are ambitious for material reward, but you don't have to have your own name in lights. Suitable jobs include anything psychological, research work, management, property and medicine.

Friends and Social Life

You make friends over a long period, and may subject them in your mind to little tests, as a way of seeing how suitable they would be for you. You most like people who are reliable and self-aware, and admire anyone who changes themselves for the bettter. Your best friends may be those who have an affinity with nature, such as a fondness for animals, plants and the outdoors. Your favourite social activities are outdoor sports, the opera, auctions, and visiting animal parks. Animals have no pretensions, and that appeals to you.

Travel and Holidays

You are adventurous in the places you visit because you like a holiday to mean something. You tend to plan it meticulously, though, and deal with any ensuing crisis swiftly and efficiently. Your idea of a good holiday is one which allows you to play native, and one which has little social contact. You are attracted to small islands, unspoilt areas, and places with rain forest. You often holiday in July.

Religion and Politics

You have strong right-wing political views, which stem from the days when you decided that the 'haves', as opposed to the 'have-nots', were those with all the power. Issues which most motivate you centre around relationships, and abuse within families. In religion you are fairly traditional, and you think that any faith which supports the family must be a good thing.

Scorpio Intuition

Yours is known as one of the most psychic signs of the zodiac, and you find it easy to accept that there are many powers beyond our current comprehension. You are very likely to have some kind of special gift yourself. You believe in self-transformation, and may be particularly interested in hypnotherapy, psychoanalysis, the tarot, and spiritualism.

Chapter Seven

RELATIONSHIPS

Compatibility – seeing eye to eye – falling in love ...
they're what make the world go round. Whether we like it
or not, we all need someone else, and there are many ways
in which we need that person. This chapter looks at relationships in all their forms. What sort of person is compatible with you? Can you do business together? Will you
be friends? Will you fall in love? Finally, for those who
wish to know, are you compatible when it comes to turning
out the lights and snuggling under the duvet together?

Astrologers are always asked to gauge compatibility
between people of differing star signs. It is impossible to
say that a person from one star sign will definitely relate in
a positive or negative manner to a person from another star
sign, but there will be certain pointers to look for, which
may lead to the ultimate success or failure of a particular
partnership.

If you are Aries, Leo or Sagittarius, yours is a Fire sign.
You will be hot-headed, impulsive and positive. You make
your relationships instantly, with no prejudice, and you
judge others by their actions more than anything. You will
be most compatible with those who allow you lots of space,
and with whom you can share excitement.

If you are Taurus, Virgo or Capricorn, yours is an Earth
sign. You are practical, realistic and trustworthy. You are
slow to form lasting relationships, and are fussy about who
you let get close. You are most compatible with those who

are sensible, sincere, and with whom you can plan a safe future.

If you are Gemini, Libra or Aquarius, yours is an Air sign. You will be intellectual, chatty and logical. You make your relationships through common interests, and you assess other people in terms of their intelligence. You will be most compatible with those who are rational, interesting, and with whom you can learn and grow.

If you are Cancer, Scorpio or Pisces, yours is a Water sign. You will be emotional, sensitive and secretive. You make your relationships often by accident, and usually through some kind of crisis – inner or external. You are most compatible with those who are quiet, contemplative, and with whom you can open up, without fear of being abused.

Love . . .

Suppose you have got as far as being in a relationship, and you wish it to work. What are the tricks of maintaining the love in your relationship, and of making sure that you are what your partner wants? After some years with the same person, what can you do to keep that initial fire alight?

ARIENS are all intense at the start of a relationship, and then they can cool off. To keep them going, make sure that you do lots of exciting things together. Never say negative things, and always be keen on their ideas. You must Dare to Do, to keep an Arien.
Love tip – Life with an Arien is for living in the here and now. Keep one step ahead of them.

TAUREANS are slow to become involved, but when they do, they are with you for life. You need to be stable, to keep your looks, and to enjoy pampering them. Money and security are important, so make sure there's always enough of both, and discuss any matters of taste before buying things for the home.

Love tip – Nothing is decided speedily, and what they want, they want. Never rock the boat.

GEMINIS are butterflies who stay with you whilst the flowers are in bloom. To make the flowering last, always have a few buds up your sleeve. Be interesting, and play hard to get at times, with a little mystery thrown in. You need to be constantly fascinating.
Love tip – If you know something they don't know, it'll keep them going for years.

CANCERIANS are home-loving people, who want to feel relaxed within their four walls. You need to show that you love them, and take care of them by doing little things that will mean a lot. Always welcome their relatives, and develop a few home-based interests.
Love tip – Allow them to dote on you, and do the same back.

LEOS are extravagant and theatrical. They will sweep you off your feet (or expect you to have done it to them), and will need to believe that you're quite a catch. Go over the top every so often, and always make space and money available for luxuries.
Love tip – They chose you because you were glamorous – don't become boring.

VIRGOS are careful about love. If they chose to be with you, they made some calculated decisions. You need to be self-aware, and to ask difficult questions at times – they will respect that. Take an interest in their health and their work, and don't be too sensitive about well-meant criticism.
Love tip – Always be seen to be responsible, and do not bury your head in any available sand.

LIBRANS are romantic. They like to be wooed and to woo, and they fell into your arms because you were gorgeous or sweetness itself. You need to have excellent manners, a charming disposition, and never let them see you looking shabby.

Love tip – Togetherness begins after all the nastiness of the world is left behind. Forgive and forget and don't let outside problems affect you.

SCORPIOS are passionate. They decide they want you, and they have you. To stay in that happy state you need to have depth, compassion and loyalty. If you risk everything for them periodically, they will give everything to you. Do or Die always goes down well.

Love tip – They want all of you, so never hold back or keep a secret.

SAGITTARIANS are extrovert. They vaguely promise the world to anyone, but if they deliver it to you, you need to be worthy of it. There always has to be an adventure, so surprise them every so often, and never be inhibited or prejudiced. They are free, and will only stay whilst you help them feel that way.

Love tip – If you love them, let them have a long rein.

CAPRICORNS are conservative, and they have definite ideas about roles. You fitted their idea of a role, and to stay in it, you need to make sure you know what they want next out of life, so that you can help them attain it. Make sure that all their friends envy them for having you.

Love tip – Find out what the most acceptable role is, and play it.

AQUARIANS are individual. They find love difficult, and often prefer their own company. If you came on the scene, it was a miracle. To keep the miracle going, be an individual yourself, and admire all their friends (there will be many). Follow every one of their crazy ideas, and only say what you mean.

Love tip – Never be shocked, and never expect to know them completely.

PISCEANS are innocents in the cruel world. They may rely on you, and you must be a rock for them to cling to. Always be strong, kind and gentle. Never ridicule them, and be wise enough to help them not to believe everything they say.
Love tip – If in doubt, cuddle them and say it'll be all right (even if you have no idea how).

The Astrological Good Sex Guide

Often misquoted as the sign with all the passion of the other eleven put together, this is only true on rare occasions. If you decide to get into lovemaking, you will be very emotional and extremely demanding, but you often have so many psychological hang-ups about sex that your iceberg cool prevents you from taking off more than your overcoat. Sex equals power never more than with this sign.

SCORPIO – In Bed With . . .

With ARIES – you are both in competition for who wants it more, for longer, and for new heights of ecstasy.
RATING . . . WOW!

With TAURUS – although you like the bull, you may find a lack of understanding that leaves you feeling cold.
RATING . . . GRIM

With GEMINI – surely one of the most surprising sexual contacts of the zodiac. You hate them, everywhere, except between the sheets.
RATING . . . WOW!

With CANCER – a real love match. They seem to care for you as much as you could care for yourself. Dreams coming true.

RATING . . . WOW!

With LEO – there are too many undercurrents for this relationship to survive, even into the bedroom.

RATING . . . GRIM

With VIRGO – you are fascinated by a person who is as obsessive as you.

RATING . . . GOOD

With LIBRA – passion will certainly be ignited by this angel on legs – it's a pity they are poor in bed.

RATING . . . GOOD

With SCORPIO – despite the reputation you have as excellent lovers, two scorpions seem to only get halfway to paradise.

RATING . . . GOOD

With SAGITTARIUS – you often need just a little push, in order to let go and make merry. Once you've been with the centaur for a while, you'll be a new person.

RATING . . . WOW!

With CAPRICORN – there's a great deal of respect in this relationship, which is good because it means you'll humour each other.

RATING . . . GOOD

With AQUARIUS – the microwave meets tinfoilperson – sparks will fly. There's no way that anything but hysteria will result.

RATING . . . GRIM

With PISCES – you will think you have landed on fantasy island when this beauty melts into your arms. Superb! RATING . . . WOW!

Quick Compatibility Guide

Nothing is trivial, as far as you're concerned, so if you decide that you love or loathe someone, it has not been a swift decision and you will stick to it. You make a fabulous friend and an evil enemy. Your greatest strength is in being loyal to the nth degree, and your greatest weakness is in taking too much too seriously.

With ARIES, you enjoy the cut and thrust of business.
With TAURUS, you find many fundamentally similar pleasures.
With GEMINI, you are shrewd enough to do business.
With CANCER, you are able to enjoy much in the way of homely pleasures.
With LEO, the business side of life works, as you respect each other.
With VIRGO, despite both being a bit serious, you can share your pleasures.
With LIBRA, they seem to be everything you'd hate to be – take care.
With SCORPIO, you should find yourself being too intense together – take care.
With SAGITTARIUS, they may offer something that you need in business.
With CAPRICORN, you like their serious approach to pleasure.
With AQUARIUS, you will feel a little undermined – take care.
With PISCES, you have so much in common that the relationship may not challenge you – take care.

Business

You are one of the zodiac's best business people. You seem to know every dodge, every trick and how to read the mind of the opposition at every turn. The only thing that you sometimes lack is courage. There are times when one should leap off the cliff, without knowing what's at the foot. If you do, with the help of a Leo or Arien, you may be surprised at how much farther you are able to travel. Sagittarians are often good for you in business, as they encourage you to be optimistic. You may – even though you might not like them – be forced to admire Geminis, as well, as they seem to be familiar with most of the tricks in your book.

Friendship

If you take pleasure at all, you do it whole-heartedly. You will not waste time messing about, and you expect your friends to be the same. Your pleasures are simple and basic, and they cost very little. Many Scorpios have firm friends in Virgos, and you have lots of time also for Capricorns. Love, when it comes, can be amazing with a Taurean, and you are also attracted to Cancerians.

Think Again Relationships

If you meet another Scorpio on a dark night, you may be mutually suspicious. Yours is not a sociable sign, and two of the same may be too much for you. You also need to question carefully how much a doting Piscean is good for you. They'll love you, but will it be a challenge?

Oops Relationships

You seem to have real problems with people who mix easily. The more friends a person has, the less you feel happy about them. You will be very wary of Librans and Aquarians.

Chapter Eight

1995
THE YEAR
FOR SCORPIO

A significant year, because it is the first of a new cycle in your life. You should feel more confident, more capable, and more in charge of your future. Any crisis will be averted, and you'll find a purpose again where previously it had been missing.

Physically, you could make a mirculous recovery from a long-standing complaint, and may defy medical opinion when you manage to make a breakthrough that they all said was impossible. This, for example, is a year in which dramatic weight loss is possible for tubby Scorpions.

Emotionally, you will have to be the prop for close relatives who are going through a difficult period in trying to accept a change. You will feel an inner calm, which is something close to having discovered a faith or belief, and this gives you a great uplift.

Family-wise, you will feel a lessening of influence from someone older, and *you* may have to look after *them* a little more. Younger relatives will need careful guidance, and one might suffer a disappointment.

Work. You are feeling as though you'd like to change career, but are you sure about it? You may feel dissatisfied with your lot, but is that a reason to run away?

Money. This year will be a turning-point for money. You should see an increase in your income, which will have lasting implications. You may now find it easier to mix with a richer crowd.

Play. There will be some difficulties in the romantic department this year, and they may lead to a feeling of resentment – something which you ought to control. Friends will be a great help.

Travel. You are unlikely to travel a great distance this year, but you may choose to visit some places near to home which are yet very unfamiliar. A holiday could be cancelled, so don't make big plans.

If Today is Your Birthday

Your year ahead is often mirrored by the events on your birthday each year. If you have a nice birthday, the chances are that it will set the tone for the coming twelve months, and if you have some problems on your birthday, perhaps they will repeat themselves in the coming year. Astrologers place a great deal of store on the planetary influences which are prominent on your birthday, or as we call it, your day of Solar Return, when the apparent position of the Sun is as it was when you were born.

October

23 This year will be about putting others first, but whilst you like to do all you can for your partner, you may have to learn some fascinating lessons in self-restraint.

24 This year will make you into a new person through enabling you to achieve goals which have not previously been accessible.

25 You will pay more attention to your personal needs, and will ensure that you get the things you most want. Be more selfish.

26 There will be some long-term investment this year, and you know that you can do great things with money, given the time.

27 This year will be very lucky for money, and you

should see your standard of living dramatically rise. Pay rises are certain.

28 There will need to be a concentrated effort to bring your business side of life up to the required standard. Make sure you do not overlook minor details.

29 You will have to learn some lessons in communication and language if you are to gain extra insight.

30 There will be a new environment for you which will be busier and more social than before. People will figure more strongly.

31 You should be looking at making a move, which will take you to a place where you will feel more free.

November

1 There are people who care about you, who would like to see you more often. Either you or they will have to make more of an effort.

2 Youngsters will need careful supervision because they are nurturing a special talent or special sensitivities.

3 There will be romance in your life, and it is likely to take you further than you expect to go . . .

4 If a younger person is keeping a secret, it could be that they are attempting to cope with everything without worrying you. Don't pry into the lives of others but do keep your eyes open.

5 You will have to work hard this year, but you should have the physical strength necessary.

6 There may be dull routines to contend with, but you will find that the more you organize your life, the more pleasure you will derive.

7 A person important to you will have to make some choices this year. There is no way that they can continue to live in the past. You will be right to encourage them to let go and move on.

8 You will find that affection is more plentiful in your life this year. A happy time.

9 Your mind will be exercised by a lively person who always tries to be one step ahead of everyone else.

10 This year will make a great difference to the way that you see yourself and your abilities. It's time to discover what you are truly made of.

11 You may find that the tactics employed by a relative are underhand to say the least. The year's family dramas will have to be seen to be believed.

12 This year will see you become much more involved in family and domestic issues, whether you like it or not.

13 It may seem a long way off, but you could be closer than you expect to finding your dream home. Do not lower your sights.

14 You are likely to be having a glamorous year, which will feature a very special holiday. Your souvenir snaps will be much passed around.

15 You have achieved success at work, so you should now be starting to delegate a little more. You cannot do everything yourself – be realistic.

16 There are specific needs that you have, which will help you to decide where you should be going with your work and career.

17 Try not to feel disappointed when a dream comes crashing down in flames. It is meant as a guide to move you in a different direction.

18 There are friends who will introduce you to a new circle this year and you will be accepted at once.

19 You will feel more politically motivated this year, and may have to stand up and be counted.

20 It will be a year of working on relationships with people who are going through difficult times, and who may be difficult to know.

21 Try being there for the people in your life who have troubles. You will become even more of an excellent counsellor than you are already.

Monthly and Weekly Forecasts

We are all affected by the subtle movements of the planets, but not all of us, of the same sign, are affected on the same day. The monthly forecasts give an overall feeling of what the month will bring; the weekly forecasts describe the influence prominent in any week, which may manifest themselves at any time during the week and may last for one day or several. The boundaries of each week may be crossed, so bear this in mind when looking at your weekly forecast.

The periods covered by each week are loosely as follows:

End one month/beginning of next	26th of one month to 4th of next
Early month	2nd to 12th
Mid month	10th to 20th
Late month	18th to 28th

January

You may have cause to regard January as something of an extension of Christmas, when the socializing seems to go on and on. You are not usually famous for your garrulous nature, but this month you'll surprise your friends.

You tend to have strong feelings about people, either liking them or loathing them. For some reason, all those you like are out in force this month. With your pals you will be indulging in games of words and exercises in general knowledge. There will also be talk of politics and beliefs, and you may have more than one heated ideological discussion.

There may be a tug-of-war in the early weeks of the year – something to do with a neighbour and a piece of property. You will stand your ground, but will you really need to?

When a friend finishes a visit you will have reached a

new understanding with them. You may, as you part, make some kind of plan which is more far-reaching than any in the past. Your friendship will be firmer.

On a matter of principle or dogma, you may have to change a personal philosophy in the light of new information being received.

You made some arrangements last year which may manage to unmake themselves this month. Any change in plan will be an improvement, so look upon this as a blessing in disguise.

There will be more invitations than there are days this month, so you can afford to be choosy.

To sum up, you will see new bonds develop this month, and should not feel wary, as they will be foundations which can be built upon for a long time to come.

End December/Beginning January

New Year, for you, is a time for getting out and about and being seen. You'll indulge in first-footing, although, the way you look, it will seem more like trick or treating. You'll probably be dressed in some kind of horrible costume.

The New Year also seems to involve making contact with certain people who may have disappeared from your life for various reasons. You may have an urge to get in touch again, or may even bump into them just when you least expect to.

There will be some letter-writing this week, and you will be waxing lyrical in a way which was not possible in the Christmas-card rush of a month ago.

You have more practical work to attend to, which may involve helping out with someone's old car. Could it be that they have a problem, and for some reason you seem to know what to do? Expect to share jump leads.

Venus is still in your sign this week and will ensure that your love life starts the year well. Expect to be kissed more than usual this New Year.

Early January

You will have a mound of paperwork to attend to on your return to work this week. In fact, when you open the door at work, it will almost seem as if an avalanche engulfs you. A considerable amount of work was shelved over Christmas, and now it all comes back to haunt you. It could be that you will have to take some of it home if it is all to be finished in time. Try not to throw valuable pieces of paper into the waste-bin.

The people around you this week will be full of talk of progress. It seems that there is a whiff of promotion or advancement in the air, and there are only a limited number of places for a particular job which everyone covets.

Friends may seem to be anything but that when there is a conflict regarding money. It may be that someone thinks that you shouldn't have what you do have, or it could be that there are other reasons for material jealousy. Try being a little less rigid in your attitude as this could be the reason for any upset.

You don't have to justify why you are spending your money in the way that you are. It may be that you have to make a large expenditure, and that is fine. Perhaps it's the attached implication which is making for a controversy.

Mid January

You may feel rather emotional for a few days this week even if you don't let it show. The Full Moon in Cancer will exaggerate feelings of loneliness which may be a current problem. You may decide to return to a place which has sentimental associations for you, or to telephone a loved one who is some distance away.

This is a strange week for travel. You may find yourself somewhere other than where you expect to be, and there could be problems connected with visiting a certain place.

Transport may also have its erratic moments, and you could have to make a cancellation at relatively short notice.

A friend may have recently been unable to understand a point that you were trying to make. Things have changed now, and you will be far more in agreement than you were.

Progress is being made with regard to a special event or competition which affects several people. The criteria for qualifying are widening, and this may be good for some people, but a problem for others, as there will be more competition. You will have cause to consider whether the widening choice is to your advantage, or whether it is time to give up hoping.

This is a good week for money, and you may be able to pay something towards a special event.

Late January

There is good news and bad news regarding something you have been looking forward to. The good news is that everything comes to a head this week and you are able to make a final choice about your future path. The bad news is that there will be a cancellation of an event which has been receiving a lot of hype and causing much excitement. You may feel cheated, but there is little that can be done.

You may hear, or be the subject of, some kind of unpleasant gossip this week. It's as though people have nothing better to talk about, and you will find yoruself feeling a bit shocked.

With regard to hopes and dreams this week, you will find yourself making some rather long-range plans, which will eventually make you a lot of money if everything happens as it should. You may choose to involve other people in them, both in terms of safety in numbers and also because you'll feel better if there are more heads dealing with one difficult matter.

There is much to be said for self-reliance this week,

and you should find that the more you allow yourself to be diverted by others, the less effective will be your actions.

February

This is a thinking month. You should always have lots of thinking time in your life – something you usually do, and when you do, you are often plotting. This type of thinking may be more to do with analysing past experiences and current form. It would seem that you are in the position of having to look both backwards and forwards simultaneously. A recent problem needs to be assessed in order for you to work out the reasons why events occurred as they did. And a future plan needs to be laid out, in military fashion, so that you won't err from the path of success.

You may be expected to know a great deal this month – almost as though you are the resident expert. It's true that you are something of a specialist in many areas, but is it fair of others to come to you with all their questions? If you can deal with them all successfully, it has to be a feather in your cap.

One question which does crop up now, is that of investment. There is talk of you having to handle a large sum of money. You may be lucky in that it could belong to you, but you may also be only the person who moves the money from one place to another. Whichever it is, the main thing to remember is that your 'hunches' are rarely wrong.

You have been exploring a new avenue recently – one which involves politics and procedures. In the past few months you will have talked a great deal about one particular subject, and will perhaps have become something of a bore about it. This month is when you discover that not all you had been led to believe was in fact the gospel truth. It could be disappointing, but at least it will firm up your own views.

You may have expected a past issue to have been sewn

up some time ago. It's nearly in the bag – but not quite – so don't celebrate yet.

To sum up, look and learn.

End January/Beginning February

The week starts with a challenge. You are likely to be asked to talk about a subject in which you will need a certain amount of expertise – something which is OK, but may prove to be more of a challenge than you first think. You do have a good deal of knowledge, but are you always able to show it off to its fullest extent?

You should reassess the things that you have decided are no longer useful in your life if you are to fully capitalize on what is expected of you. You have almost thrown away an item, or at least consigned it to the loft, which is exactly what you need to have next to you. Try rooting around in your effects.

The New Moon will sow a seed inside your mind. It may not manifest itself straight away, but in the next few weeks you will have cause to look back on this time as the point when you first started to change. The change is most likely to be in the area of your inner needs. Why should you contine to fight against something which is a natural process of evolution?

You have been dealing with extravagance recently, and there may still be reasons why you have to be the voice of economy, crying out in the wilderness of financial profligacy.

If you have dreams of being recognized for something that you have achieved at work, try and plan your strategy carefully this week, because you do stand a good chance of success.

Early February

This is a week for give and take. You are usually good at both but sometimes get them mixed up. You need to make sure that you are being totally fair. If you are perceived by anyone not to be fair, you may suffer from the negative opinions that this will generate.

You know more than you let on this week – especially with regard to a person who is putting on a brave face, despite feeling quite sad. You may be able to take them on one side and show them that you know what's really going on – it could be a comfort.

The family are being quite difficult, which is nothing new. What is new is that it is reaching ridiculous proportions, and soon somebody will get quite hurt. Maybe you need to intervene slightly and show them that you do care what happens at home, even if they feel that this is not the case.

This is a week for sticking to your guns and for making it quite plain that you have no wish to be diverted from your ambitions. It could be that others have been thinking that you have been easily swayed. In fact, this week makes you more clear than ever about what it is that you most require.

Take some time to be with a brother or sister this week – they'd appreciate it.

Mid February

This time of year always seems to be symbolic of much more than just Valentine's Day. It could be that you are about to make a change at home, and you are using the positive atmosphere that often can prevail at this time as a way of softening an announcement which you plan to make. This week is not really that calm, though, and you could be blamed for making things worse if you try to introduce any reform.

It is likely that for once the general consensus at home is behind you. That should surely be a good thing, but it will take some time before you are able to make the changes that you wish. The next few weeks will prove to you that you were right all along in making certain assumptions.

The Full Moon occurs at a time when you are trying to make a big impact. You need to march into a room and take over but may well be finding this a difficult move. People seem to be only just able to understand what you're talking about, and you'll have to tone things down so much more if you are to gain popular understanding. Try not to aim too high too soon.

The family will seem not to understand what you are doing at work, and may almost seem to be trying to pull against you on a professional matter. You could have to back down when you had been wanting to pursue one goal in particular.

Late February

The Sun moves into Pisces and takes with it a feeling that you have to teach others what you have learned. You will wish to stand up and be counted, and will make a point of showing what you consider to be the right way to certain people who you really feel should be taking note. You will, if you are involved in any kind of instruction, be expected to know everything.

There will be some kind of signing off, or finishing off, going on this week, and it will have a financial flavour to it. You could be putting the finishing touches to a material project which has been in the pipeline for some time, and you may need the assistance of a financial professional, like an accountant.

At home, the atmosphere is improving, and it almost seems as though people are being kinder. If there is an older relative with whom you have been embroiled in a long-term misunderstanding, you may well be able to see the situation improving from now on. It's as though they have suddenly started to be realistic in what they expect of you.

If there are holiday plans at the moment, make sure that you have all the costs in front of you before committing yourself to something which could be much more expensive than you imagine.

March

This month may feel somewhat strange to you. It's as though part of you is missing. An old way of life might have come to an end, and it seems to have taken something from you. Alternatively, it could feel as though a very uneasy calm has developed. It's almost too calm. The silence may be deafening, and that in itself may worry you. You're not a great one for trusting – always wanting to be in control of things yourself so that you can have the final say. Perhaps what this month teaches you is that by learning to appreciate this quiet time, you will understand why personal space is necessary to you and everyone else.

You do like to make an impact, and so this month you will not be as compliant as you might be at other times. In reaction to the way in which you may feel you have been cheated of something that was rightfully yours, you will be likely to express yourself as though someone owes you something. Perhaps this is a good time to look inward, and to ask yourself if you couldn't be just a little kinder.

You have good reason to feel confident at the moment – especially with regard to the material side of life. You have been saving up for some time – hoping that your ship would come in. That ship is now all but in, and you should be starting to reap the benefits in no time at all.

If you have been chasing promotion at work, or looking for a new avenue of expression, you may have found it. You are one of the few people who understands how to fix something which is actually a very expensive item and which could be easily damaged. Security and safety suddenly become your two middle names.

To sum up, once you get over your initial resentment

this month, you will be much happier about your chances of being accepted in the way you would like.

End February/Beginning March

You will not be able to believe just how dim other people are at the moment. You are the only one who seems to know how to solve certain difficulties, and if those difficulties extend to fixing something that is broken, your expertise will count for everything.

The New Moon may not coincide with any great changes in your life, but one thing that will be significant at this time is the way that you are more able to make your point through your creative endeavours, transforming something dull into something charismatic. It may take some time to achieve all this, but it has its roots in this week.

You have a burning need to get on and do the things that are most important to you, at the moment, and if that means making time for work in what is usually your home schedule, you will do it. Not everyone at home may agree with the way that you so easily sacrifice your supposed free time.

Early March

There is talk of a journey, and it may be something to do with that old cliché 'across the water'. As ever with good clichéd fortune-telling, you should be wary, because all is not what it seems. The only thing needed to complete the picture is the proverbial mysterious stranger! There will certainly be unfamiliar people around, but they're probably not so much scary, as irritating.

It's more easy than might be imagined to spend money at the moment. You should be feeling confident financially, but that very fact may be what makes for a few difficulties this week. You could be overly generous, but it won't have the desired effect – the more you donate, the more you will be asked to give.

People are all too keen to talk this week, and that may be something to do with the fact that they are slightly short of things to do. If this is the case, the more time they have, the more they will idle it away chatting about subjects that have very little to do with them.

You know what needs to be done, so why are you so incapable of getting on with it?

Mid March

This week will be one which contains a few good laughs. You will be intrigued by the carefree attitude of younger people. This refusal to take life too seriously can be an uplifting experience, and this is certainly the way that you allow yourself to experience it now.

The Full Moon will see a friend experiencing a crisis of control. They are one of those people who need to have everything 'just so' and unfortunately this is not possible this week, with the result that they feel their finger is no longer on the pulse.

You may need encouraging to abandon your past beliefs this week. What is the point in clinging to something which no longer represents the way that things are today? Others who care about you can see the difference, but you may take a long time to accept the fact.

The pressure to be at home and to be quiet is strong at the moment, and it could get to the stage where you need to have a day or two away from your usual routine, as a way of getting your head back together.

Late March

With the Sun moving into Aries you are more inclined to feel energetic. You may choose to look at yourself in the mirror and decide that it's about time that your body had an overhaul, as it is looking as though it's been asleep for a hunded years. Sport and exercise may therefore feature a little higher on your list of priorities, and you may decide that it's about time you put yourself under a regime which will test and possibly punish you.

There will be good news at work this week. You may find that a long-running series of difficulties will be cancelled out by a new broom which is embarking on a vigorous clean sweep.

The family may have some kind of get-together this week, and it will be bigger than is originally envisaged. You will enjoy feeling part of a greater whole, and may allow the more rowdy members of the clan to take all the limelight.

A journey to a place high up, perhaps in the mountains or a city with high-rise buildings, will be significant this week. You will observe that a situation is finally at an end, and you may be able to bury something at last.

April

One thing that really bothers you is other people calling the shots in your life, making you feel powerless – and, as a result, frustrated and resentful. This month may change all that, when you find yourself building up a certain amount of resistance against those who you feel have pushed you around in the past. If you've been a Scorpionic worm, you'll turn, and there will be no telling what you might do next.

Your partner is the one who is most likely to attract all the flak from any great build-up of emotion. They may be to blame, it's true – they could be the one who caused you to feel the way that you do – but they might, just as easily, be the one who gets in the way when you are spitting out venom.

Things will have to change at home, and you may launch into older members of the family with your own idea about what they should be doing, or not doing, in relation to you. They may, of course, take it much better than you dread they will, and the chances of this happening are really quite high. You in turn may be the recipient of their frustrations and longings, and the air could end up generally much clearer.

There is also a struggle at home with younger members of the family, who seem to think they are much older than their age would suggest. They feel quite sure about their decisions, and quite able to look after themselves – something which you would tend to query.

Luckily, away from home things are going well. You have money in the bank, and work seems to be improving. You can look forward to having a much happier time in these areas in the future.

To sum up, problems at home need attention, but you may find that by creating a storm, everything feels so much better.

End March/Beginning April

This week is one in which work will assume great prominence. There are important jobs to be done, and you will have to rush them to a certain extent, as the longer you leave them the greater a problem they become. It will be OK to launch into things, but you will find that if you think about matters for too long, you will get yourself into a mess.

With Aries being strongly represented at the moment, it is likely that you will need a challenge this week. Try not to take on just anything that is offered to you – you are in the mood for a fight and will need to tackle a job which is demanding and physically taxing.

There will be some news on the financial front this week. You may be disappointed when a promised source of income is either not forthcoming, or vastly reduced from the potential that you thought it once showed.

You care about public opinion at the moment, and will court it wherever you feel it to be most useful. It's not that you're licking boots, but you are keen to be seen to be supporting the most acceptable points of view this week.

Early April

You will make a trip this week to see some relatives. There may be a reason behind your visit, other than merely a duty call, and you could be intending to make a point which cannot be held back any longer.

The financial news is better this week – especially if you have been hoping that your recent efforts at work would pay off. Pay off they certainly have, and in the next few days you will receive confirmation of what you have been hoping for.

The way that you dress is significant this week. Our clothes often communicate something about us to observers, and you must get across the right message. Take extra care when putting your image together, and remember that you have to show that you are 'with it', without being too exaggerated.

It's not always that easy to be totally separated from the prevailing moods this week. If you were hoping to have a purely objective approach to your situation at the moment, you may need to think again. What you see as an unbiased opinion is really much closer to one-sidedness.

Mid April

When Libra is emphasized you often become more introvert, and eclipses have a strange effect on everyone, so when a Full Moon Eclipse occurs in Libra, as it does this week, you will feel most peculiar. Over Easter you may easily feel like retiring from view because something that you always believed in has been taken away from you. Where in the past you may have found some spiritual solace in the whole message of Easter, this week it will seem to be just a façade.

Mercury moves into your opposite sign, Taurus, and this will emphasize the way in which you relate to other people. You need to sit down and discuss the most significant issues, and will perhaps be having a few meetings so that certain tactics can be thrashed out.

Someone will come to you with a problem, and you, in turn, may have to refer that problem to a higher authority. If there is some kind of emotional situation, you will need to tackle it very carefully.

Late April

The Sun moves into Taurus this week and emphasizes much about your closest relationships. It's as though you have reached the stage where you need more from your partner, or are prepared to commit more of yourself to your partner, and it will be a useful time for building for the future.

At home, there will be a few reasons why someone's behaviour is in question. You may feel that it's OK for certain people to be thoroughly unconventional for much of the time, but when it comes to their behaviour selfishly affecting everyone else, the time is right to tell them that enough is enough.

You need to put on something of a show at the moment, and may have trouble in getting your partner to understand just how much certain situations mean to you. They may be swift to criticize and slow to empathize with your needs, and could be totally contemptuous of the circles you are attempting to mix with. A tense atmosphere prevails.

May

You may feel as though you have trodden a particular path many times before, when you are asked to do it again this month. You could be standing in for someone at work who should be replacing you, or you could be helping out an old love, in a way that their current partner should be doing. Don't look at this month as a step backwards, but do look at it as one of the last times such a thing will be asked of you.

In your love life, things have moved on in recent times, and you will have shared with your partner some highly emotional moments which may, in fact, continue during this month. You know what needs to be said, and you will say it – regardless of the way in which it could be interpreted by those observers who seem so interested in everything that you and your partner do.

At home, you will feel as though you are having to play host to an alien figure this month when a person comes into your life who represents something that you are very much opposed to. You could, for example, be a vegetarian, and your daughter brings home her new boyfriend, a slaughter-man. Rest assured that the situation won't last and that equilibrium will be restored before too long.

A friend made a promise to you ages ago that you had thought they were going to break. The good news is that they come up trumps this month and present you with a *fait accompli*, which means that not only do you have what you wished for, but you don't have to do any work for it, either.

To sum up, the month is one of some emotion, and you may find out more clearly than you expect just who is to blame for what, and who, on the other hand, should be trusted.

End April/Beginning May

This week is all about helping your partner with the jobs that are currently needing to be done. You may feel lacking in some of the skills which are asked of you, and could be learning some new tricks of the trade as you go. If you are doing anything outdoors this week, you will be glad of the fresh air.

The New Moon will coincide with a change of plan for

the coming weeks. It will become clear that what you had originally planned will now no longer be feasible. It will lead to a rethink, and you will be looking much more practically at your own and others' skills when trying to create a more workable situation.

There will be a message or some news this week which will throw a spanner in certain works. You may feel as though you have to teach a dog how to chase a rabbit, when someone asks you for some guidance. You find it incredible that they should seem so slow in understanding something which should come as second nature.

You'll continue to feel this week that those nearest to you are being a little too keen to push themselves at work, and you may have to make some rather large allowances for their behaviour. You perhaps will acknowledge that what's right at home is not right at work, and vice versa.

Early May

This week brings you a little closer to understanding the inner workings of the mind of a certain close member of your family or close friend. One or maybe more very useful conversations will help to clear some air between you.

You may be involved in buying or selling this week – especially in the working arena. You could find yourself making a great effort to either convince a certain person that they need a commodity that you have, or that they really want to let you have something of theirs. You could be shopping, for example, for a significant item and see just the thing, but with some sort of hurdle between you and it. It all goes to make the week somewhat challenging in places.

At home, there is talk of breaking free. It is likely that you will observe someone's move towards independence, and it could take a form which is disturbing to those who always want life to be static. If it's you who's being stubborn, ask yourself what anyone except you has to gain by it.

Mid May

The Full Moon is in your sign this week and starts the week off with a drama which you will have to overcome before anything else can happen. You may be dealing with high finance, but it could just as easily relate to the emotional state of a loved one – something which is rather volatile. You'll find that the best way to deal with your emotions at the moment is to allow the expectations of others to call the tune.

With togetherness as a workable theme at the moment, you will find that most activities seem better when you are sharing them with someone else. There may be a tendency for you to lean on a particular person, but it would be foolish of you to do so all the time. You need to stand up for your own needs, but bear in mind that support is there, if you require it.

For the past few years May has brought you some tough twists of fate to deal with, and this month will be no exception. There will almost be an irony in the way that a personal situation turns out this week.

Late May

The Sun moves into Gemini, and you'll be glad of the chance to confront a person or situation which has been getting to you for some time. There will be a shift of emphasis this week, from having to deal with day-to-day niceties, and not being able to get past them, to dealing with more fundamental issues of understanding, sharing and working together on a project of some magnitude. If you have recently set up a business venture, you will find that this week should see an end to the petty bureaucracy and you will now be able to get down to the real work.

It's like getting blood out of a stone when you sense a crisis in a loved one and are trying to get them to talk it through. You will be faced with jokes, off-the-cuff remarks and changings of the subject, all designed to stop you from penetrating their armour.

Mars changes signs, and it indicates that you are keener to be seen with the right people, as well as doing the right thing. If your views are asked for, you will be happier to express them than maybe you were in the past.

June

Why is it that the past won't stay buried and forgotten? You had just got used to the idea that things were starting again for you, when all of a sudden someone from the past crops up and lets you know that they remember things you had rather were forgotten. Your reaction to such a revelation, apart from horror, is to decide to put paid to the tittle-tattle, once and for all. You will have to use some fairly plain speech (but you are good at it) if you want to be taken seriously.

You do fear being unable to contain certain people around you, who seem to be determined to make things difficult. It's not to say that they are being deliberately awkward – it's more likely that they are acting naturally and for some reason you are interpreting their behaviour as being far more devious than it is. You must keep yourself in check, if you have no wish to be seen as the villain of the piece.

There is a gold-mine of money for you waiting around the corner, and one way in which you can get nearer to it is by opening your mind to new ideas. If someone was to say that you could be rich, if only you would allow yourself to think more broadly and be more open, could you do it? It's all out there – get seeking.

You may feel that youngsters are taking up a great deal of your time this month, but interestingly they are having a positive effect. In keeping up with what they think about, you are being youthful and positive in your approach. If faced with difficulties at this time, ask yourself how someone ten, twenty or thirty years younger would deal with them.

You may be toying with the idea of joining a special interest group. You will do so soon, and should make sure that you know the relevant details.

To sum up, try to be lighter and brighter in June.

End May/Beginning June

You'll start the month by relying heavily on your partner. It's not that you want them to organize your life for you, but if you don't allow them to be close to you, and to be an influence now, then when will you ever? Love is a strong motivating factor at the moment, and you will make a point of ensuring that others see how much you do love certain people.

The New Moon will bring out the more inquisitive side to your character. You know that there are things going on that perhaps no one really knows about, but you will not accept that ignorance is bliss in this particular case. You will ask questions and will make a point of finding the answers. There are continuing difficulties in the business world at the moment, and you will be feeling quite irritated by the way that a job is not being done. You will have very little patience with organizations who are messing you about, and if you are having anything to do with bureaucracies you will be ready to climb the wall. There is, however, nothing that can be done, and you will have to wait a good few weeks before you get results.

Early June

You will be introducing your partner to a friend or acquaintance this week, and they will have much in common, particularly in one specific subject you know nothing about. You may observe both being highly practical and sensible, and may feel that you could do with learning some of their technical awareness.

There are no further steps forward in a business matter this week, and you may be inclined to think that there will never be any joy. If writing a letter would make you feel better you should do so, and it might assist you in getting your point across in the end.

There will be a worrying few days in which someone you know seems to be going through a particularly stressful time. It may be their health or it could be that their mental state is giving cause for concern.

Rely on the things that your partner is saying and you won't go far wrong. Although they may not fully understand exactly what you're going through, they are sensitive to the situation.

Mid June

The Full Moon will identify a financial crisis. It may not affect you personally, but it does look as though you will have to intervene in a situation where money is the key factor. Whilst not necessarily linked, any business problem that you may have been experiencing could start to change at about the same time.

With Merury turning to face the right way now, you may find out the truth about some kind of delay which has been holding up a particular plan. You will realize that you have been given a different story from someone else, and it will make you see everything clearly for the first time in weeks.

Venus moves into Gemini, and your partner will start to change their entrenched idea about something that you hoped they would see sense about. Their approach will be different from your own and you may feel that they lack the staying power necessary, but what you do like to see is that they are now being more adaptable.

Late June

With the Sun in Cancer you will feel more comfortable, and may be able to make yourself more at home in what could have been, up until now, an environment that is slightly alien. You will find connections between places and people you know today, and places and people from your past. You may be wondering why you are almost reliving a past event.

There are continuing business activities at the moment, and you may be in a much better position than you have been for some time. There are much more helpful conversations to be had with certain contacts, and it may be that you will be able to further resolve any outstanding differences of opinion.

Your friends will be slightly agitated this week when a relationship starts to break up, or is found to be fatally flawed. It may take some time to deal with, and you could be needed in a crisis-counsellor role.

If a loved one is going on a trip this week, you will be pleased for them, even if you can't claim to be thrilled at their choice of travelling companion.

July

You're a great one for pulling back the curtains of life so that the truth can be seen. This month, it may prove to be too difficult for you to pull back anything, as there are some quite entrenched blockages which are not easily dislodged. You may sink your teeth into what you feel needs to be done, but will you get anywhere with it? It looks as though you won't.

To be philosophical about it, you should use the time that this gives you to examine your motives. It's not easy to sit back and pull yourself to pieces, but that may be all you are able to do in the face of a series of events – possibly seemingly unconnected – which conspire to dismantle what you have been trying to achieve.

At home, younger people seem to know more than they are admitting to, and there could be some kind of intrigue going on – something which no one has bothered to tell you about.

This month will have its fair share of dramas, and they will mostly involve friends, rather than you directly. You will have to help someone through an entanglement in their love life and another person who is involved in some kind of business deal which is getting too much for them.

Your opinions, always so firm, are often kept in the background because you have no wish to cause trouble deliberately. This month, however, the turn of events is such that you find yourself making an issue of something that you feel is quite against the normal way of going about things.

There will be times this month when you are shopping for some kind of special gift for a loved one. You will find just what you want in a very unusual place.

To sum up, this month you should keep your ear to the ground, as well as a wary eye on the door.

End June/Beginning July

This week is one in which you will see it as your role to clear up everyone's messes. It's about time that someone sorted out certain pressing matters and you will feel that this needs a person who can stand complications – i.e. yourself. If a visit to the hospital is called for, you will have to get on with it. The same can be said for the dentist. You may find yourself ferrying a friend or relative to such places more than once this week.

The New Moon will take you back to your birthplace. You will be pleased when a relative makes you feel very much at home and, in some ways, it's as though you never left.

You will be working in some kind of group situation this week with a common aim. You will have much to say about your goal, and will perhaps feel that you are not being specific enough, as a group, in your plans. It's a good time to narrow your focus.

Early July

This week will see you involved in an endless series of discussions. It is debatable as to whether any of them will come to fruition. You know that to certain of your friends and colleagues, the topics under the microscope are new and exciting. To you, however, it is much truer to say that you feel that everyone is expecting your expertise to hold the situation together. You don't mind being relied upon, but not all the time.

Venus moves into Cancer, and it will bring you a pleasant few days away from home – possibly making a visit to a place that you remember from years ago. You will have a sentimental tear in your eye at something that really triggers off a past experience.

Saturn is being troublesome this week, and it will cause you to be concerned about the welfare of a younger relative, who may be backtracking on a sensible career step.

The Full Moon at the end of the week will have an effect in your neighbourhood in some way, and could mean that you will be boasting to your neighbours – or they will be boasting to you – about a possible new car.

Mid July

Mercury joins the Sun in Cancer briefly this week, and it is likely to bring out the travel bug in you. You don't like to go too far, but you do like to go to places which are deeply significant. If travelling to a place where there are lots of old buildings, you will enjoy yourself.

You may get the feeling that certain people in charge at work are trying to cut corners and finish a task ahead of schedule. If that is the case, you will become quite angry because their motivation is slightly selfish, to say the least.

With Mars in Virgo making a powerful angle to Pluto in your sign, this week, you will decide that you need to have a new social life. This will be a good time for trying out different forms of entertainment. If you like things which test you, you may choose something along those lines.

There will be some sadness attached to news which comes from a city this week. It seems as though it is the end of an era for someone you know who has to give up an old way of life.

Late July

The Sun moves into Leo, making you much more assertive. You want to go out into the world and be dynamic, and you don't see why anything should prevent you. This is a very positive time for making a big impact and you will start right now.

Mercury also moves into Leo this week, and that in itself will ensure that current projects stand a much better chance of success – especially if they involve you as a lead figure. You need to be free to make decisions which will affect the running of an organization, and if you are in middle management, you must be alllowed by your bosses to make policy decisions affecting those for whom you are responsible.

Mars moves into Libra this week, and you will use that influence to help you to communicate with people who perhaps are a little more delicate than yourself and with whom you have to behave in a circumspect manner. You can be very tactful if necessary, and you will need to be now.

August

In the last few years, you have really been through the mill when it comes to dramas. This month, one final problem looks like clearing itself up – thus allowing you to feel that you now know just what is expected of you and where you should be heading in the future.

Your confidence should start flooding back soon, and you may feel that it is necessary to make some obvious changes to your lifestyle, particularly your image. This is a good month for finding bargains in shop sales, having all your hair cut off, growing a beard, or whatever makes you feel good and different.

You have had the feeling – perhaps all year – that 1995 is somehow different for you and in August it may begin to show. People will start to notice that you have changed, as they say, and will start to tell you how well you're looking. Try not to put on excess weight at this time, by the way.

You could be the one person who is representing some kind of stability in a business situation, at the moment. It may be that you are involved with people, on a professional basis, who are saying one thing and doing another. This will prove to be most irritating, but you'll cope with it, as long as they realize that they can't fool you.

Quite unexpectedly, you will be asked to join a club or committee this month, and although you might have initial reservations, you will find that it is thoroughly satisfying.

Finances are looking good for August, and you'll be keeping an eye on investments – possibly making one or two very sensible decisions.

To sum up, you are almost like a butterfly taking its first tentative steps out of its pupa.

End July/Beginning August

The month starts with some good news about work and your ambitions. You discover that you are in the front-running for some kind of advancement or promotion, and it will mean that you can start to feel much more confident. If this possible job has anything to do with being in charge of something – i.e. management, or the running of your own set-up – you can afford to be really optimistic.

Venus moves into Leo, and that may be just the incentive you need for making headway in impressing all the right people. You will find that your popularity rating is on the way up and that you'll make some sort of public contribution to a group effort.

By the end of the week when the Moon is in your sign, you should know one way or the other about your prospects. Your intuition is usually strong, so why worry? You're bound to know what's going to happen anyway.

Early August

This week sees the beginning of the final stages of your planet Pluto's move through Scorpio. This will prove to be one of the turning-points of your year, and you will have much about which to be glad. You will perhaps feel that events from the past few years are now reaching culmination and the time is most definitely right for moving on, and for making plans for the future.

Mercury enters Virgo this week, and it will see you hard at work trying to convince certain people of how important it is to take steps to rationalize a procedural matter. You feel that there has been much too much waste for far too long.

The Full Moon will see you making time to be at home, but it is important that you have someone to stay with you at the moment. A friend is likely to visit and you will enjoy their ability to communicate.

Mid August

This week will see you trying out some new plans or arrangements, and they will involve personal changes. You will be keen to alter your appearance at the moment and may be looking at some different types of clothing, or a new hairstyle.

You'll have much to do with the people from work, and someone in particular will be an endless source of fascination for you. You may meet a hypochondriac, who will tell you in detail about every ailment that they have ever suffered. In one way, you will find this most interesting, and in another way, you see them as some sort of psychiatric case. If you have anything to do with the medical profession, look carefully at what is behind the things this person is saying. You may be on the verge of a breakthrough in knowledge.

Late August

This week will see the Sun move into Virgo. As it does, it will emphasize your analytical side and will cause you to ask a large number of questions. You are one of those people who finds it really easy to extract information out of the people you meet, and this week, by bringing in a few well-chosen thoughts, as well as by watching very carefully what is going on, you will learn a great deal.

Venus moves into Virgo this week as well, and it will bring with it a host of invitations. You will not be invited to anything trivial, and you will be required to participate in an event when you get there.

After doing so well in the work stakes this month, there may be a disappointment coming up. It could be because you have tried to be in too many places at once, or it could also be that there is someone in a lofty position who feels that you are trying to usurp their throne.

September

You are known as being the silent sign of the zodiac – the person who sees and hears all, but who reveals nothing.

A dilemma may face you this month. You are party to some information which will alter the lives of certain people near at hand. Do you keep it to yourself, or is there a moral obligation to reveal the truth? This may be a question which preoccupies you for much of the month. You have no wish to upset certain applecarts, but maybe it would be for the best if you spoke up.

Love is a tricky subject for you, because you find it very hard to take it lightly. This month you will be faced with a particular problem: should you make it plain how much you feel towards a certain person, or should you try and swallow your feelings and think about something else? You may not get any help making a decision in this area. It will be tricky.

You could say that one of the reasons why you are in this situation is because you take everything so seriously. Is that a bad thing?

Life is definitely moving into a new phase these days, and you will find it far less easy now to make choices about the future. It's almost as though someone is dealing you a new hand of cards, but only one at a time. It makes it very tricky, therefore, to make any long-term plans.

There will be good news about money this month, and it will be news you'll want to spread. It's nice to see that some things in life are reliable.

To sum up, you have to make a change soon, but you can't do it yet.

End August/Beginning September

You will have much to do this week, which is just as well, because if you have to think about things too deeply at the moment there may be some kind of brain explosion.

The Moon passes through your sign and it will make you more aware of the needs of others. In fact, you seem to know their minds so well, that it will feel a bit scary.

You will have a heap of secrets to keep this week. This could be because you work in a profession where you are not allowed to talk about your work, or it could be because you have been confided in by a loved one who has sworn you not to tell the very person you are most likely to talk to.

There is a question of territory this week. You may feel that the issue of personal space is what's really behind a certain person's claim that someone has encroached too much into their area. Are you a referee in this situation, or merely an interested observer?

Early September

Mars slips into your sign this week, and you will feel that what has been needed for some time is a little home-truth-telling. There are reasons, however, why it is prudent to say nothing at this time, no matter how much you may be bursting to.

Your charisma rating is shooting up at the moment, and a person who you hardly know may find that there is more to you than meets the eye. You may be flattered by any attention, but does it mean that this situation is going to develop into anything more intense?

Chiron moves into Libra, marking a week when you have almost run out of sympathy. You cannot cope with many more sob stories, and you are reaching the point when you think that your friends save them all up deliberately, in order to make you depressed.

The Full Moon will bring a bright spark in the shape of a young and innocent relative, who makes you realize that everything is so worthwhile really.

Mid September

You may be wondering just how much longer a person you see every day is going to go on pretending that black is really white, and that they are happy when it is patently obvious to you that they are not. This may be the only way that they know how to deal with a certain relationship problem, and whilst it makes you feel tense, surely their main priority in this is self-protection?

You will have something to do with putting people together this week, and there may be a professional way in which you are able to unite two parties who need something that each other offers.

A younger person is in need of support this week. It looks as though they are taking a perfectly natural situation far too seriously. It may be a first love or first rejection which is taking its toll of them.

There is likely to be a surprising meeting in a strange place this week. You will bump into just the person who is able to offer an insight into your situation from a detached point of view, and you will be very grateful.

Late September

The Sun will move into Libra this week, and this is often the time of year when you feel most in tune with the difficulties and frustrations of others. You have already been experiencing enough of this this month, and may now be reaching the stage where you need to stop the world and get off for a while. You require a break and some time to consider your own needs above those of others.

Mercury starts to backtrack in Libra this week and it will confuse certain situations for you. It is easy to misjudge things at the moment from your step to a business matter. You are well-advised to take extra care when walking in the street, or driving the car, and also to look before you take anything approaching a leap in business.

The New Moon at the end of the week will hopefully afford you a little space so that you can put up your feet and relax.

October

The spiritual side of life has always been important to you but you have tended, at times, to neglect it in favour of more pressing and more earth-based demands. You may feel guilty about this, and will try to redress the balance wherever possible. This month may be one of the occasions when you can make some changes.

If you have been too involved with the problems of the immediate family, you are more likely to put them out of your mind in October so that you can look at the needs of a wider group. It would seem that you are quite motivated by a social cause which, to some people, is less than attractive. You will do your bit this month, and may allow your own idea of God to influence the way in which you handle certain situations.

You have little time for selfishness at the moment, and may be appalled at the way that some people, particularly those who are younger than yourself, are behaving. It's almost as though the more they have, the more they want, and it upsets you.

For many months, you have been seeking answers to fundamental questions which may be quite hard to put into words, such as why there is sickness in the world, and why people have to starve. The questions are so big that the answers take a long while to arrive. This month, possibly because you are working with those who need your help, you will find the answers to difficult questions, perhaps alongside some personal truths.

Your finances are such that you could be thinking of making an important expenditure this month. Is it anything to do with a new car?

To sum up, you will have much to think about in

October on a spiritual level and some may wonder just how long it will be before you become a missionary!

End September/Beginning October

This week will see you spending some time on causes of a worthy nature. You'll find that you have greater sympathy for those in need, and there may be a particular problem, connected with the breakup of a relationship or a family, that you feel deserves your attention.

Mercury moving backwards in Libra makes the week somewhat difficult to accept, in places – you feel that people are being less reliable than they should be. When you discover that a so-called friend has lied to you, you are likely to be quite hurt.

The Moon is in your sign at the start of the week, and it will make you aware that certain things are coming to an end. The week will have an element of finality about it.

There is good news about finance, but it may not affect you as much as it does another person – partly because you are not at all sure that you want the responsibility of sharing the available resources with those who most need them. You must do it, however, as people are relying on you.

Early October

The Full Moon Eclipse will cast a shadow over your working life and you may be feeling that it is every man or woman for themselves. There is a possibility of redundancies or sackings this week, and whilst they probably won't affect you directly, you may have to sympathize with the way that a vulnerable person, possibly someone on long-term sick leave, is being treated. Make sure you tie up any loose ends because it looks as though certain chances are just about gone, and any Scorpio in a dodgy work situation may have to expect the worst . . .

95

Venus moves into your sign this week, smoothing over any rough corners you have been experiencing. You may feel that a recent misunderstanding which gave a friend totally the wrong impression of you can now be cleared up. You will find that others are far more ready to give you the time to fully explain your point.

Uranus and Neptune change direction for the better this week, and whilst you may not notice any immediate improvement in a business situation which you have been hoping will go in your favour, at least you can now see that there will be no further deterioration.

This is also a good week for the development of your mental faculties, and if there has been some kind of frustrating intellectual question hanging over you for some time, it seems that you will now have a better chance of making a valuable and creative contribution to the topic.

Mid October

The big change this week may not be outwardly apparent. The week is all about coming to an inner understanding or acceptance of a matter which has been playing on your mind. You may have had questions about self-worth recently, and could have been asking yourself whether there was any point in going on in certain areas. Your answer will come from an unexpected source. Someone totally uninvolved may help you to see where a compromise is needed.

You may take a slightly dim view of the goings-on at work this week. If there has been some kind of bust-up, you will be left feeling that certain people are much colder than they might appear, and that if you were in their shoes you would not be able to live with yourself. It is easy, however, to be both over-emotional and irrational at the moment, and perhaps there needs to be a little more understanding on your part – even though to ask such a thing is somewhat unreasonable.

Late October

With the Sun entering your sign this week you will feel as though you are at last making some headway in your working and business interests. There will be an end to the double-talk that seems to have been coming from certain sources for much too long, and you will feel that some of your views are at last being taken seriously.

Mars leaves your sign this week, and it will inspire you to get on with making inroads into a new area. If you are looking for someone to recognize your talents, you will have to be quite assertive in the way that you market yourself to them. And if you feel that you are unhappy with the way you look, why not spend some money and splash out on a new outfit, or go on a diet, or choose to give up smoking?

The Solar Eclipse falls in your sign this week, and it marks a turning-point which has been a long time in coming. You will be writing down some new ideas, and also daring to try things which you have never tried before. From now on there needs to be not just a new you, but a you which is *seen* to be new.

November

You will be very pleased when you start to see progress in a matter of an official nature which you have been pushing for several months. At last people in positions of so-called power will start to take notice of your point of view. You know how to pull strings and it looks as though you have been tugging the right ones.

How many people do you know who are vulnerable and in need of protection? You may immediately think of the family, and indeed, if any of them were likely to be threatened in any way, of course you would do something about it. It's more likely, though, this month, that the people who need your support are those who are seen as being a threat themselves – particularly to society as a whole. You may have chosen to get yourself involved in working with a disadvantaged group, like drug addicts or homeless people, and in this area you will feel very protective.

If you are involved in organizing some kind of special event for your birthday, make sure that you have plenty of plans in reserve. It's likely that what you initially want to do will not be possible. If you are not involved in the organization don't expect to really enjoy it – you won't.

One other thing about birthdays. This year's birthday is not that exciting, but what it does represent is the passage of time and the old way of life finally coming to an end. You have moved on, and will continue to do so.

As if entertaining wasn't bad enough, you'll have a hefty bill to pay this month. It's as though you're having to finance your own treats. Try not to be the one who's buying the drinks all night.

Your taste for the finer things of life could get the better of you this month, but don't expect your money supply to be infinite. It will run out.

To sum up, the 'meaning' of life is changing.

End October/Beginning November

This week is one of those times when, wherever you are, you feel as though you should be somewhere else. Traditionally at Hallowe'en all the spooks are supposed to come out and dance, and many Scorpios have moments when they feel about as welcome as a ghost in the house. You may feel that people are slightly afraid of you or what you stand for, and this week may involve you in having to mix with all those people who are slightly apprehensive about your motives – thus making your position uncomfortable.

You are good at dealing with people, and this week you will be presented with a situation which would worry lesser mortals – i.e., you will have to help out a group of people, or an individual, who is seen by others as being slightly disreputable. You will manage it well, though.

With Venus currently in your sign, you will be filled with good feelings about the future. You can see that your hopes are coming true in the way that you wish them to, and this will make you highly optimistic about your path in life. Make the most of feeling so good.

Early November

Venus leaves your sign this week, and it will leave you with a happy feeling of confidence in your ability to do something that you have been aiming at for a while. If you have been expecting some money to come in, it will materialize around about now.

Mercury moves into your sign this week, and brings some long overdue information to you. You have probably been waiting for weeks and weeks to hear about a business matter, and at one stage it may almost have seemed to be cancelled altogether. At last, however, the news is good, and was worth waiting for. If any of this is to do with a legal expert, it may be more understandable – if not any more acceptable.

The Full Moon will remind you that you cannot force a horse to drink, even if you have coerced it to the water. You may be dealing with a relative or colleague who is so determined not to move that they have virtually fossilized, and you could find yourself having to rethink tactics.

Mid November

This week will have its emotional moments, partly because you are one of the few people who really understands the depth of pain or regret that a loved one is going through. It could be that you will be the person they confide in, and whilst you are very moved by their situation, there is very little that you are able to do, except comfort them.

There will be a contact with an institution this week. It will probably be a large organization like the Civil Service or the BBC, and you will receive some good news from them. You may have dealings with older people, as well, and there could be a connection between the two.

You are not known for your adventurousness and daring, but this week a reckless gambler may pop up where the model of restraint used to live. You will take a chance with a financial matter, which will pay off in quite a specific way. Others may marvel at your technique.

This is a week for speaking the truth. If anyone needs to be put in the picture, this is the moment for it to be done. Make sure you spell out exactly what they need to know.

Late November

Before everything slips into Sagittarius this week, the New Moon will happen in your sign. This will represent a second chance to do something that you thought you had missed. It will be possible to retrieve an item or situation that you had thought was lost, and it will also be possible to redress the balance in a matter which you had been feeling was left hanging uncomfortably in mid-air.

Saturn in Pisces will emphasize the changes that are happening in the life of a young relative this week. Whilst you will not be able to help them, at least you will be able to see that they are making what has been a long overdue, but correct choice.

There will be many occasions when money is discussed this week. You will not necessarily have to spend more, but perhaps the expected bills which come in will be slightly higher than they should be and it will stretch your resources.

The month closes with a decisive step which could not have been taken even a few weeks ago. You will feel quite sure that you are doing the right thing at last.

December

1995 comes to an end, and takes with it more than just the past twelve months. You are a person who always looks deeper for the implications of your actions and the meaning behind events, and this month even more so.

The past few years have been a time of some deep thinking. If you compare yourself with how you were in say, 1988/9, you will see that your grip on philosophy and the meaning of life is now much clearer. You seem to have a greater life purpose these days, and will be able to explain your beliefs to your friends and family alike. Indeed, it might almost be argued that you have developed a tendency to preach to people, but this is only because you are so passionate about your recently found faith.

On a more mundane level, 1995 has provided security in a way that has been somewhat lacking in recent years. This Christmas's present-shopping will be all the easier for knowing that you can safely afford your purchases, instead of having to scratch around to find enough money to pay for your goods.

There will be time to complete a particular task this month – despite the holiday season creeping up on you all too quickly. You will have the required patience to do the job.

This month will call upon some of your practical skills, and you should find that you will be able to show certain cowboy-type tradespeople a thing or two. By outplumbing the plumber and outstitching the tailor, you will save yourself some expenditure.

1996 will be a year of investment in the future. You will be talking about shares and pension schemes, and will have an eye out for some investment-type property or commodities.

End November/Beginning December

Venus in Capricorn will ensure that the Christmas shopping frenzy starts now. You cannot prevent it creeping up on you from now on, and you are likely to get on with the job of producing a worthy Christmas for the family, starting now.

Mars in Capricorn will make you a little more serious about your shopping this year. There will be a definite plan, and you will follow it to the letter. You believe in purchasing gifts which are exactly 'right' for certain people, and you will not stop until you find the thing that you feel is appropriate. You will be particularly interested in books and literature this year, and in devices and gadgets which may be antique or have historic connections.

There is a decision to be made this Christmas and it is far-reaching. It may have much to do with you personally, and is difficult to actually talk about with many people, but it is something that will alter your life quite considerably. You have changed a lot, but this one thing will affect the way in which you relate to many different people in the future.

Early December

There may be parts of the Christmas celebrations that leave you cold. You are a person who likes there to be meaning in the things that you do and experience, and you can't help feeling that the true significance of Christmas is swept aside in the face of commercialism.

This week is a week in which you will feel under more stress than perhaps you should. One could almost say that some of it is self-imposed. You may feel that other people seem determined to ignore you and your needs, but this could not be further from the truth, if only you could see it.

The Full Moon will make it likely that you have to attend some kind of meeting at work, and it will be the sort of meeting at which tempers could flare. Certain people may say rather too much about their opinions and you need to be one step ahead of any criticism of your department. You are not wrong to go in on the attack if you feel that those dishing out the criticism are taking a highly superficial view.

Mid December

Mercury moving into Capricorn is likely to make you feel rather tongue-tied when it comes to putting on some sort of show. There may be expectations which will lead to your having to give some kind of speech or introductory pre-amble, and you will feel grossly unequal to the task. There may be an issue which needs to be resolved between you and a relative. If so, you will still find it hard to get started with the things that need to be said.

Shopping will continue this week, and you will feel that it is worthwhile going into the expensive shops if the service is better. Why should you stand in crushing queues when you could be in a relaxed environment down the road?

There will be time this week to look for a few bargains, despite perhaps searching in expensive areas for them. You will have one extraordinary piece of luck, which will make you feel very special.

Late December

The Sun moves into Capricorn and you will be talking in terms of doing your duty by certain people you know. You will probably call in on neighbours and relatives who you feel might not otherwise receive many visitors over the holiday, and you will perhaps invite someone from outside the immediate circle to join in with your Christmas.

Venus in Aquarius heightens all the usual family tensions which seem to be ever-present, and you might have to adopt the role which you never see as rightfully yours – that of arbitrator. You always seem to have to step in and pour oil over troubled water, and you may reach the point when you say that you would rather let everyone get on with their petty squabbles.

You do feel for some people outside the family who are not having a pleasant Christmas. In fact, so strongly will you feel about the underprivileged that you may choose to make quite a sacrifice in order to ease what you see as the collective guilt of the majority.

Chapter Nine

MOON MOODS

Statistics show that the moon, the closest heavenly body to the Earth, has a special effect upon life here. It has an orbit around the Earth of twenty-eight days – a lunar month – and it passes through all twelve signs of the zodiac in that short period. It spends about two and a half days in each sign every lunar month.

Our behaviour is affected quite closely by the phases of the Moon. At a Full Moon, i.e. when the entire disc of the moon is visible from Earth, it is said that accident and crime statistics rise, animals behave in a disturbed manner and all our bodily fluids are more volatile. Similar trends are recorded when the Moon is New, i.e. invisible from the Earth, as the shadow of the Earth entirely covers the moon, but the New Moon is said to have less dramatic effects.

The two-week period between the time when the Moon is New and when it is Full is called the waxing cycle, and the two-week period when the Moon appears to shrink from Full back to invisible to begin at New again is called the waning cycle.

Occurring halfway, at seven days between New and Full is the First Quarter Moon, and its opposite number, seven days between Full and New, is called the Last Quarter Moon. The Moon's cycle, then, can be divided into four main quarters, one occurring every seven days. It's now easy to see why we have seven-day weeks – they tie in with the Moon phases.

Each Moon phase has a different meaning. If you can take advantage of the prevailing trends when making decisions, it can help you to lead a more successful life. A waxing moon is considered to be helpful for change, and a waning moon is considered to be a consolidating influence. Farmers often plant by the moon. At a New Moon it is easier for plants to grow and a Full Moon is the best time to harvest. Start your new project at a New Moon and plan your major events for a Full Moon.

Below you will find a list of the meanings of the Moon phases and the dates when these phases occur. Following that, look at how the Moon works in individual star signs, and plan your activities in accordance with the nature of the position of the Moon.

New Moon

This is a time of new beginnings. In the seven days following a Full Moon the seeds of ideas are easily born, plans come to mind and the past can be put behind you. This is a propitious time for starting a new course, job, relationship or research project.

First Quarter

This is usually when ideas become reality. In the seven days following a First Quarter Moon activity is the name of the game. This is the right time to push yourself to the front of any queue, to ask difficult questions, to embark upon a new diet, to spice up your love life, and to enter competitions.

Full Moon

The Full Moon is often active before it occurs, so allow a couple of days ahead of the date for its influence to show, and it will last a good week after its exact date. This is the most dramatic time of any month, and is the time when pots boil over in all sorts of areas. People embark upon affairs, make marriage proposals, and often get pregnant during this period. This is the most likely time for arguments, resignations, strikes, revolutions and violent acts. If you want a wild time, plan it for a Full Moon – parties are eventful, noise is everywhere and your sex appeal may be brimming over. It's a question of harnessing the power – or it will harness you.

Last Quarter

This is the time of the month when we start to calm down. In the seven days between Last Quarter and New, tradition prevails. This is the best time for sentimentality, for practicality and for authority. Choose this time for filing, catching up on a backlog, and for saying sorry to all those people you may have offended.

Below is a list of the dates when the various Moon phases are exact. You will also need to check the sign in which the Moon falls, so that you can ascertain the particular nature of the individual Moon.

New Moons

January	1, in Capricorn	March	1, in Pisces
	31, in Aquarius		31, in Aries
April	29, in Taurus	May	29, in Gemini
June	28, in Cancer	July	27, in Leo
August	26, in Virgo	September	24, in Libra
October	24, in Scorpio	November	22, in Sagittarius
December	22, in Capricorn		

First Quarter Moons

January	8, in Aries	February	7, in Taurus
March	9, in Gemini	April	8, in Cancer
May	7, in Leo	June	6, in Virgo
July	5, in Libra	August	4, in Scorpio
September	2, in Sagittarius	October	1, in Capricorn
			30, in Aquarius
November	29, in Pisces	December	28, in Aries

Full Moons

January	16, in Cancer	February	15, in Leo
March	17, in Virgo	April	15, in Libra
May	14, in Scorpio	June	13, in Sagittarius
July	12, in Capricorn	August	10, in Aquarius
September	9, in Pisces	October	8, in Aries
November	7, in Taurus	December	7, in Gemini

Last Quarter Moons

January	24, in Scorpio	February	22, in Sagittarius
March	23, in Capricorn	April	22, in Aquarius
May	21, in Aquarius	June	19, in Pisces
July	19, in Aries	August	18, in Taurus
September	16, in Gemini	October	16, in Cancer
November	15, in Leo	December	15, in Virgo

The Moon travels through the entire zodiac every twenty-eight days. When the Moon is in particular signs, it favours particular activities. If you are a betting person, you may find that the characteristics of the sign of the Moon are mirrored by the success of a particular race horse, football team or contestant.

The element of the sign that the Moon is 'in' will indicate the type of activities most likely to be prevalent. Fire signs make for active days, Earth signs for practical days, Air signs for social days, and Water signs for emotional days. When the Moon is in your own sun sign, it is usually a turning-point for you, regardless of its phase.

ARIES MOON will be a busy time, with lots of confrontation, physical energy and enthusiasms.
Betting tip – Look out for names to do with fire, war, vitality and beginnings – also the colour red.
Health tip – A time when it is easy to become overtired and stressed.

TAURUS MOON will be a time of building and shopping. The necessities of life, like food, clothing and money are important.
Betting tip – Look out for names to do with food, nature, animals and the earth.
Health tip – A time when your system may be sluggish, and when your throat may be tight.

GEMINI MOON will be a time of communication and movement. Books, magazines and journalism will be emphasized.
Betting tip – look out for names to do with words and language, abbreviations, initials and anything humorous.
Health tip – A time when you may be feeling nervous or excited, and could easily strain your eyes.

CANCER MOON will be an emotional time, when people will talk about the family, the home, the past and domestic pursuits.
Betting tip – Look out for names to do with history, the family, women in particular, and any emotions.
Health tip – It's easy to worry at this time, creating nervous stomachs. Try and relax.

LEO MOON will be the time for leadership and glamour. Show business, management and most creative pursuits do well.

Betting tip – Look out for names to do with royalty, the theatre, wealth and gold.
Health tip – You may be more likely to strain your back or raise your blood pressure at this time.

VIRGO MOON will be the time when practical pursuits are most popular. Work, organization, realism and the simple things of life all matter greatly.
Betting tip – Look out for names to do with jobs, efficiency, computers and short, to-the-point expressions.
Health tip – A good time for fasting or dieting as your system will reject any toxins now.

LIBRA MOON will be the best time for making peace. The Arts will be emphasized, and so will love and marriage.
Betting tip – Look out for names to do with relationships, anything arty, and also deals or agreements.
Health tip– It's easy to overindulge at this time. You may have a craving for sugar.

SCORPIO MOON will be the time when dramas come to a head, when you are faced with tough decisions, and when life can seem to be cruel or emotional.
Betting tip – Look out for names to do with controversial subjects like death, sex, religion and power.
Health tip – Listen to what your body is really telling you, and don't do anything dangerous.

SAGITTARIUS MOON will be a time of expansion and progress. Luck is considered to be a driving force here, and there is great optimism.
Betting tip – Look out for names to do with foreign countries or people, jokes, or anything to do with risk-taking.
Health tip – It's easy to get carried away and to miss out something important, like a meal, or your usual tablets.

CAPRICORN MOON will be a time of direction. Plans are

important, and the future is discussed. Convention and tradition succeed here.

Betting tip – Look out for names to do with success, rocks, high places, and business. Important colour – grey.

Health tip – Not a good time for bones, teeth or skin. You may discover a rash, or feel a rheumatic pain.

AQUARIUS MOON will be a time of science. Anything technical will be in evidence. Also popular will be politics and unusual people.

Betting tip – Look out for names to do with people, politics, machinery, or anything futuristic.

Health tip – Your circulation will need to be maintained at this time, so no crossing of the legs for long periods.

PISCES MOON will be a sensitive time, when people will easily be emotional, and when psychic or spiritual matters will be in evidence.

Betting tip – Look out for names to do with water, mysticism, innocence and institutions.

Health tip – You may feel strange without knowing why. A good point to spend time away from other people.

Dates when the Moon is in particular signs
Note that the Moon changes sign at a precise moment. For the sake of convenience, the main sign in which the Moon falls on any day is the one included on the chart on the next page. It is possible that the influences from the adjacent signs may be felt on some days.

	JAN	FEB	MAR	APR	MAY	JUN	JUL	AUG	SEP	OCT	NOV	DEC
1	● ♑	♓	● ♓	♈	♊	♋	♌	♎	♐	☽ ♑	♓	♈
2	♑	♓	♓	♉	♊	♋	♍	♎	☽ ♐	♑	♓	♈
3	♒	♓	♈	♉	♊	♌	♍	♏	♐	♒	♓	♉
4	♒	♈	♈	♊	♋	♌	♍	☽ ♏	♑	♒	♈	♉
5	♓	♈	♉	♊	♋	♍	☽ ♎	♐	♑	♓	♈	♉
6	♓	♉	♉	♊	♌	☽ ♍	♎	♐	♒	♓	♉	♊
7	♈	☽ ♉	♉	♋	☽ ♌	♎	♏	♑	♒	♈	○ ♉	○ ♊
8	☽ ♈	♊	♊	☽ ♋	♌	♎	♏	♑	♓	○ ♈	♊	♋
9	♉	♊	☽ ♊	♌	♍	♎	♐	♒	○ ♓	♈	♊	♋
10	♉	♊	♋	♌	♍	♏	♐	○ ♒	♈	♉	♊	♋
11	♉	♋	♋	♍	♎	♏	♑	♓	♈	♉	♋	♌
12	♊	♋	♋	♍	♎	♐	○ ♑	♓	♉	♊	♋	♌
13	♊	♌	♌	♍	♏	○ ♐	♒	♓	♉	♊	♌	♍
14	♋	♌	♌	♎	○ ♏	♐	♒	♈	♉	♊	♌	♍
15	♋	○ ♌	♍	○ ♎	♐	♑	♓	♈	♊	♋	☾ ♌	☾ ♍
16	○ ♋	♍	♍	♏	♐	♒	♓	♉	☾ ♊	☾ ♋	♍	♎
17	♌	♍	○ ♎	♏	♑	♒	♈	♉	♋	♌	♍	♎
18	♌	♎	♎	♐	♑	♓	♈	☾ ♊	♋	♌	♎	♏
19	♍	♎	♏	♐	♒	☾ ♓	☾ ♈	♊	♋	♌	♎	♏
20	♍	♏	♏	♑	♒	♈	♉	♊	♌	♍	♏	♐
21	♍	♏	♐	♑	☾ ♓	♈	♉	♋	♌	♍	♏	♐
22	♎	☾ ♐	♐	☾ ♒	♓	♉	♊	♋	♍	♎	● ♏	● ♑
23	♎	♐	☾ ♐	♒	♓	♉	♉	♌	♍	♎	♐	♑
24	☾ ♏	♑	♑	♓	♈	♉	♊	● ♎	● ♎	♏	♐	♒
25	♏	♑	♑	♓	♈	♊	♋	♌	♎	♏	♑	♓
26	♐	♒	♒	♈	♉	♊	● ♋	● ♍	♎	♐	♑	♓
27	♐	♒	♒	♈	♉	♋	● ♌	♍	♏	♐	♒	♓
28	♑	♒	♓	♈	♉	● ♋	♌	♎	♏	♑	♒	☽ ♈
29	♑		♓	● ♉	● ♊	♋	♌	♎	♐	♑	☽ ♓	♈
30	♒		♈	♉	♊	♌	♍	♏	☽ ♐	☽ ♒	♓	♉
31	● ♒		● ♈		♋		♍	♏		♒		♉

● New	♈ Aries	♌ Leo	♐ Sagittarius
☽ First Quarter	♉ Taurus	♍ Virgo	♑ Capricorn
○ Full	♊ Gemini	♎ Libra	♒ Aquarius
☾ Last Quarter	♋ Cancer	♏ Scorpio	♓ Pisces